and the Nuclear
Option

Escalation and the Nuclear Option

BY BERNARD BRODIE

PRINCETON, NEW JERSEY

PRINCETON UNIVERSITY PRESS

1966

Printed in the United States of America by
The William Byrd Press, Inc., Richmond, Virginia

Dr. Bernard Brodie, formerly of the graduate faculty of Yale University and subsequently a Senior Staff Member of The RAND Corporation, has now returned to the academic world as Professor in International Relations in the Department of Political Science, University of California at Los Angeles. He was also a member of the original faculty that organized and opened the National War College in 1946, and was later a member of its Advisory Board. He has been a frequent lecturer at the several service war colleges of the United States, and an occasional lecturer at the National Defence College in Canada, the Imperial Defence College in London, and the NATO Defence College in Paris.

He is the author of the famous and widely used STRATEGY IN THE MISSILE AGE and A GUIDE TO NAVAL STRATEGY, both of which have gone through multiple editions and translations. Also among his books are *Sea Power in the Machine Age* and (as co-author) *The Absolute Weapon* and *From Cross-Bow to H-Bomb*. He has edited and co-authored a volume published in Paris, *La Guerre Nucléaire*.

Preface

THE MAIN body of this book, that is, the part following the Introduction, was written for the major clients of The RAND Corporation while I was still a staff member of that organization. It was my original intention to develop and expand each of the several sections of that piece, after it had served its initial purpose for the Air Force, so that the final product might have been a substantially larger book. However, the processing of the original piece, including the necessary clearance review, took so much time that I decided that for publication purposes I had better stay with what had already been "cleared," while making any essential additions in the form of a separate piece, which is in fact the present Introduction.

The reader is perhaps advantaged thereby. To expand is not always to improve. As it is, the book has less weight, can be read faster, and is cheaper to buy.

By the time I came to write the Introduction, I had accepted an invitation to return to the academic world. The change meant, among other things, that clearance on new material ceased to be a requirement—though naturally I still bear responsibility for matters of security, and I have in fact voluntarily sought and obtained competent criticism in this respect. However, although the review authorities have never been unfair with me, there is inevitably a certain lightening of the spirit during writing which comes from knowing that any criticisms of government policy I might be moved to make will not have to be reviewed for clearance by persons who are identified with that policy.

The paper added as an appendix was one I read before the American Psychological Association in September 1964, in a panel which bore the title: "Pacifism, Martyrdom, and Appeasement: Dealing with Intractable States by Non-Violent Means." Because it was never published elsewhere, and because I felt it to be decidely germane to the main subject of this book, the publishers and I agreed that it lent itself for inclusion here.

ACKNOWLEDGMENTS

In the various stages of the preparation of this book I have received critical comments, some most valuable, from the following: Herbert S. Bailey, Jr., John R. Boettiger, Harvey A. DeWeerd, Herbert S. Dinerstein, Alton Frye, Paul Y. Hammond, Arnold L. Horelick, Fred C. Iklé, Victor G. Jackson, William Jones, Roman Kolkowicz, Marvin M. Lavin, Nathan Leites, Robert A. Levine, Theodore M. Parker, Thornton Read, Thomas C. Schelling, Bruce L. R. Smith, Robert M. Smith, Kenneth C. Strother, and Thomas W. Wolfe.

May 1966
Pacific Palisades
California   BERNARD BRODIE

Contents

Escalation
and the Nuclear
Option

Introduction

HONESTY MAY not always be the best policy, pragmatically speaking, but it is usually commendable. Let me therefore state at the outset that this book—though I hope it is respectably analytical and even objective—presents an argument. I have tried to be fair to opposing arguments, but I have been conscious of taking part in what may loosely be described as a debate, one in which the other side has had an astonishing success both among students of strategic affairs and among those responsible for determining United States official defense policies. Inasmuch as I have been engaged in this debate, partly through various other published writings, for more than three years, I may even hope with this piece to take my leave of it—though the subject is bound to continue to be important for a long time to come.

My part in this controversy can hardly be one to give me great satisfaction. For one thing, I have found myself obliged to defend the idea of using or threatening to use tactically what J. Robert Oppenheimer has recently called "that miserable bomb." Who can enjoy finding himself in a position which, besides being somewhat lonely intellectually, seems by contrast with that of the opposition to be more than a little insensitive, heartless, and even wicked?

There is irony in it too, for I have been opposing a position which—as the record shows—I played a special part in helping to create. Early in 1952, when the thermonuclear bomb was not yet a reality but known by a few of my RAND colleagues and myself to be clearly in the offing, I began to urge in what were then highly classified writings and briefings the related but distinct ideas that in a thermonuclear age we must seek means of limiting war, even between the superpowers, and also of avoiding too exclusive a dependence on nuclear means of fighting.

Trite as such notions seem today, they were not so then. To express them openly and repeatedly, one needed the fortitude to be willing to appear something of a crackpot—even within the RAND organization itself. Oddly, the ongoing Korean War appeared at the time to have little effect on strategic thinking, partly because of the momentum of strongly entrenched axioms like "all modern wars are total wars," and partly because our top military leaders thought the Korean War to be, through most of its critical phases, primarily a Soviet *ruse de guerre* designed to draw our military forces into a distant and insignificant theater while the Russians prepared to launch aggression in Europe! Following the Korean War there was the famous Dulles "Massive Retaliation" speech of January 12, 1954, reaffirming United States dependence on its strategic nuclear power.

Even as late as the Quemoy crisis of 1958, few of our combat aircraft had bomb-racks suitable for carrying "conventional" or non-nuclear bombs.

President Eisenhower is reputed to have been advised by the Joint Chiefs that if we intervened we would have to do so by nuclear means, inasmuch as we had, allegedly, insufficient conventional capability. There had, after all, been the Eisenhower-approved "New Look," in which the decision had been made that since the United States "could not afford" to sustain large nuclear capabilities and also substantial conventional ones, we had to go nuclear all the way.

There could be no doubt of the correctness of coming down on the nuclear side *if* the choice needed to be so drastic and far-reaching, but there was much reason, especially in view of our great and growing wealth, to believe that there was no such need. My own writings and briefings at the time were consistently critical of the official views and policies of the time, which I held to be excessively obsessed with general nuclear war.[1]

---

[1] My own relevant initial writings, beginning in January 1952, were in the form of RAND "Ds" (i.e., internal "documents"), briefings, and memoranda, as well as lectures at the several United States war colleges. These papers were then highly classified (because of references to thermonuclear weapons not tested until November 1952, and not publicly announced until 1954), and though they have since been declassified they were never published. My first openly published articles on these matters were: "Nuclear Weapons: Strategic or Tactical?", *Foreign Affairs*, XXXII (January 1954), 217-229; "Unlimited Weapons and Limited War," *The Reporter*, November 18, 1954; and "Strategy Hits a Dead End," *Harper's Magazine*, October 1955, pp. 33-37. The ideas of these papers were developed further and published in book form in my *Strategy in the Missile Age*, Princeton University Press, Princeton, 1959, especially ch. 9. The story of these and other persons' contributions is told to some extent in Morton Halperin's *Limited War: An Essay on the Development of the Theory and an Annotated Bibliography*, Harvard University, Center for International

Now, times have changed, and the big change came with the inauguration of the Kennedy administration in January 1961. By that time, ideas of limited war and of non-nuclear fighting were very much in the air. President Kennedy, who as a senator had avidly interested himself in these matters, even to the point of reading a good deal of the relevant current writings on these subjects, came into office with some ideas firmly fixed in his mind. As Richard E. Neustadt has put it, one of President Kennedy's "three main purposes in office" was to get "the nuclear genie back in the bottle."[2] He also had a deep concern with nuclear "proliferation," which was obviously connected in his thinking with the obligation to reduce our own dependence on nuclear weapons for resisting aggression. In his Secretary of Defense, Robert S. McNamara, he not only found a dedicated and loyal servant but also one who from independent influences was more than ready to fall in with the same philosophy.[3]

Surely all civilized persons must share in greater or less degree a desire to put the nuclear genie back in the bottle—though we should also recognize that like the classical genie of legend it has

---

Affairs, Occasional Paper No. 3, May 1962. However, Halperin seems not to have examined unpublished, though widely circulated and available papers.

[2] See his "Kennedy in the Presidency: A Premature Appraisal," *Political Science Quarterly*, LXXIV (September 1964), especially p. 325.

[3] I have described some of these influences in my review article on the book by W. W. Kaufmann, *The McNamara Strategy*. See "The McNamara Phenomenon," *World Politics*, XVII (July 1965), 672-686.

done some useful service, such as critically reducing the probability of war between the United States and the Soviet Union. It has with almost equal certainty—unless we play the game very foolishly —also greatly reduced the probability of large-scale war between China and the United States. These are no small services, and it is essentially the main purpose of this essay to plead for keeping and indeed expanding the benefits that have come to us from that same "miserable bomb"— which would be bound to stay with us anyway.

What, then, *is* the argument about? In essence, it is about the cost and possibly even danger of carrying an intrinsically good idea so much too far, and with so much excess of fervor and religiosity, that it becomes a crippling obsession. These are admittedly loaded words, but I believe the following essay will indicate why they do apply both historically and also currently to certain American views, including obviously official views, which inhibit unduly our capacity to use—or, much more important, our capacity effectively to threaten to use— nuclear weapons on the tactical level. It is fair to say that we have come close to depriving ourselves of a real tactical option in nuclear weapons, despite the fact that Mr. McNamara appears to be more than usually devoted to expanding "options."

This self-denial may indeed be a good thing for reasons other than those usually advanced, and if so it would not be the first time that a sound conclusion has followed in the train of (though it can hardly be derived from) bad reasoning. In the following essay I shall confine myself mostly to the situation that has confronted NATO in Europe, and almost entirely to the arguments usually advanced for building up conventional forces in Europe as a *substitute* for reliance upon tactical nuclear weapons. Although this controversy seems at the moment to be in abeyance, it is far from dead. The arguments I have in mind center mostly around the allegedly self-propelling escalatory effect of any use of nuclear weapons.

I shall have relatively little to say about the proliferation issue, which is of course closely related. But if we are going to relinguish reliance upon tactical nuclear weapons in order to help restrain proliferation, we ought (1) to be clear that we are doing so—as opposed to remaining in a state of confusion about it—and (2) to have a better idea than most of us do today about what price we are prepared to pay to buy how much anti-proliferation restraint. It happens to be not at all obvious that extreme nuclear restraint in our own strategic planning will be of critical help in restraining proliferation.

Incidentally, I should make clear that what I have above referred to as a "debate" or "controversy" deserves such a label only as a sort of intellectual courtesy. There has in fact been a conspicuous lack of any real debate. We must remember that the number of persons in this country who are responsible for developing the leading ideas in the strategic thinking of our time, though considerably greater than it was a dozen years ago, is still very small. It is even smaller, very much smaller, abroad. Thus, an idea can often win what looks like overwhelming acceptance simply because the number of literate and articulate people who need to do the initial accepting is small, and they may therefore relatively easily be brought to apparent consensus. They happen to know each other personally, and usually have much shared experience.

That has certainly been the case with the "conventional war" idea, and, as I have already suggested, the protagonists of this idea have had a fantastic success with the policy-makers of the country at least since the beginning of the Kennedy administration. The military have been on the whole—in varying ways and degrees, depending partly on individual differences and experience but largely also on the branch of service involved—opposed, resistant, or ambivalent to the idea; but for a variety of reasons, including required avoidance of public recalcitrance, have not been especially articulate about their views. The real opposition has come from our NATO partners abroad, but this has been stimulated far more by political and economic than by intellectual considerations.

As a result, the issues have been most grossly drawn. Questions of how tactical nuclear weapons are to be used, of what size, in what numbers, against what targets, and especially under what circumstances, have been hardly at all discussed publicly. On strategic issues as fundamental as these, one suspects from long experience that a lack of public discussion usually reflects also a lack of real rumination on the relevant subjects within classified studies. By now we can say that almost no one disputes that some substantial conventional capability is necessary to a power like the United States or to an alliance like NATO. Contingencies have occurred and will no doubt continue to occur in which resort to or threat of tactical nuclear weapons is by almost universal consent unthinkable. Where there *is* lack of agreement and where there *should* be active controversy concerns mostly the kinds of circumstances warranting readiness to use such weapons—circumstances which should be appropriately anticipated in contingency planning.

In an article published in the spring of 1963, I quoted from the current version of Secretary McNamara's annual book-length Statement before the Senate Subcommittee on Department of Defense Appropriations to indicate the goals the Secretary then seemed to entertain for the further building up of our own and especially allied conventional forces in Europe. These goals seemed to me inordinately high, for a number of reasons that I set forth in that article, and I urged that the pressure to achieve such goals was, in view of the attitudes of our allies, impolitic and unwise. I suggested also that the emphasis ought to be rather on making more efficient, in terms of combat readiness, the conventional forces already existing in

Europe, perhaps even at the expense of reducing their number if our allies were not going to increase their budgets, as I then thought would prove to be the case.[4]

Then and in the intervening time, I have been sometimes admonished by various colleagues—apart from the far more numerous group who disagreed outright with my views—that I was "beating a dead horse," that the Secretary of Defense had never relinquished the idea of using tactical nuclear weapons to the degree that I had apparently attributed to him (or at least to those who prepared his public papers for him).[5] It is true that the open American vocal pressure upon our allies to build up their conventional forces began to relax in 1964, and by 1965 it had apparently disappeared. However, that change was mostly the result of the realization that our allies were simply not going to

[4] This paper, "What Price Conventional Capabilities in Europe," was originally published in *The Reporter* for May 23, 1963, pp. 25-33. However, since it contains several points not repeated in this book—and in fact makes only one side reference to the escalatory question which is the main thesis of the present work—I might add for the convenience of those who might wish to consult it that it has been reprinted in a variety of places, including the British journal *Survival*, v (July-August 1963), 148-155; Henry A. Kissinger (ed.), *Problems of National Strategy*, Praeger, New York, 1965, pp. 313-328; Bernard Brodie (ed.) *La Guerre Nucléaire*, Editions Stock, Paris, 1965, pp. 203-222; and Fausto Bacchetti, *La Strategia Nucleare*, Edizioni di Communità, Milano, 1964, pp. 418-436.

[5] As I indicated in the above-cited review article of the Kaufmann book, a comparison of Secretary McNamara's prepared statements—which obviously have to be constructed under his supervision by his staff—with his spontaneous replies to questions in congressional hearings often show considerable discrepancies of outlook.

2

INTRODUCTION

meet our demands in this respect. On the contrary, some of our most faithful allies, especially the British, began to talk about reducing rather than increasing their conventional forces in Europe.

Even so, in the most recent of Mr. McNamara's annual reviews to the same Senate subcommittee, that of February 1966, after inserting (p. 37) the usual reminder that the number of tactical nuclear weapons in Western Europe had continued to increase—this time the figure was "about 85 percent" during "the last five years"—the Secretary made the following statement:

Theater nuclear capabilities are a necessary complement to but not a substitute for *non-nuclear capabilities which are large enough to meet and withstand a major Soviet non-nuclear assault in Central Europe for a reasonable period of time.* [Italics added.]

Shortly following that was another statement:

It is not yet clear how theater nuclear war could actually be executed without incurring a very serious risk of escalating to general nuclear war.[6]

Other statements immediately following in the same document confirmed the general view implied

[6] Both these statements are on page 79 of the mimeographed version, released to the press, under the title: "Statement of Secretary of Defense Robert S. McNamara Before the Senate Subcommittee on Department of Defense Appropriations on the Fiscal Year 1967-71 Defense Program and 1967 Defense Budget."

in the above-quoted remarks. Also, Under Secretary of State George W. Ball observed on April 10, 1966, that the French withdrawal from NATO might force the West to use nuclear weapons "earlier than we might otherwise do" in a world conflict, such an outcome being "conceivable because we are removing a part of a defense in depth which is useful."[7] One was justified in concluding that if the pressure upon our allies had been relieved for pragmatic reasons, there had not yet been any real change in conviction in the upper reaches of either the Department of Defense or the Department of State.

It is the fate of every book dealing with current issues that it must at some particular moment of time go to press, and it is the fate of this one that it goes to press at a time when events seem, at least on the surface, to make its entire message far fetched. In Southeast Asia we find ourselves deeply involved in a war in Vietnam, which, whatever other lessons one may derive from it, seems by almost universal agreement to have no place for the use of tactical nuclear weapons. On the other side of the world the blows of President de Gaulle against the concept and even the viability of NATO seem to put a low order of priority on any discussion of specific NATO strategy for Europe.

However, it would be totally misleading to accept such a conclusion. For one thing, a book on issues of strategy should rarely deal exclusively or

[7] *New York Times*, April 11, 1966.

even mainly with the here and now, if for no other reason than that any novel message the book may happen to contain takes too long to be accepted and digested—if such is what it deserves. Another and more persuasive reason is that it has to deal with events which may be long delayed, or happily never take place at all.

If we grant that the continuance of NATO as a viable and flourishing alliance and institution has been important to the United States—though it was surely wrong to encourage the Europeans to believe it was more important to us than to them— then that continuance was more important by far than the ideal correctness or the economic efficiency of its military planning and arrangements, about which our government has been so exercised. That was one of the chief reasons I actively opposed views which seemed to me not only intrinsically wrong, and thus actually contrary to economic and military efficiency, but also seriously disturbing to the coherence of that alliance. At any rate, if there were serious errors in NATO planning, they seemed to me (and to various others) to be posed not in terms of *how* best to meet a massive Soviet attack but rather in terms of whether that was the kind of crisis we really ought to be chiefly worrying about as compared to much lesser crises. On the other hand, in so far as we do have to have some concern with it in planning terms—from the point of view of SHAPE, considerable concern with it—it has always seemed to me the condition that posed practically no difficulty *in advance* between adopting a nuclear or a non-nuclear tactical posture. As will be seen in the following essay, that part of my opposition to the "conventional war" idea about which I feel the least doubt concerns its applicability to a massive, and thus deliberate, Soviet attack.

We are not here concerned merely with winning debating points, but there is some reason to consider that the U. S. position on conventional forces played a part in provoking President de Gaulle's impatience with the Organization.[8] Certainly the American position had been closely connected with an all-too-vocal and even hectoring opposition to De Gaulle's nuclear ambitions, an opposition that persisted long after it should have been clear that the General was not going to be in the least dissuaded by it. No doubt this diplomatically clumsy because futile intervention annoyed him. Also, our continued emphasis on building up conventional forces in Europe obviously helped to confirm the French suspicions—certainly not confined to De Gaulle or even to the French—that they could not really depend on our nuclear arsenal's being used in their defense. However, I do not wish to pretend that these elements likely played the major role in the highly disruptive attacks that President de Gaulle was inflicting on NATO in the

[8] That happens to be the view, for example, of the veteran Paris correspondent George W. Herald. See his "The Stakes for de Gaulle," *The New Leader*, March 28, 1966, p. 6.

early months of 1966. He no doubt had other reasons, the primary one being that he felt safe enough no longer to need our "leadership," which in any case he did not enjoy.

Our main dilemma in Vietnam was neatly phrased 400 years ago in the two halves of the admonition in Polonius' famous advice to Laertes:

> Beware
> Of entrance to a quarrel, but, being in,
> Bear't that the opposed may beware of thee.

An American intervention that was meeting so much opposition in the world at large, including the United States itself, where it was especially meaningful to our government, was no place to start using tactical nuclear weapons. The high involvement of the intellectual community was also significant far beyond its proportionate showing in the usual public opinion polls. The fact that the most clamorous part of the opposition was largely pre-empted by those who were almost totally ignorant of the character of the Viet Cong or of the real nature of the "National Liberation Front" (which is not to say that the few relatively well-informed were of one mind in support of administration policy) had practically nothing to do with the case. Tactical nuclear weapons could in any case probably have had only a marginal (though doubtless technically positive) tactical value.[9]

[9] I must anticipate some questioning of the parenthetical re-

Nevertheless, the great residual value of our nuclear power, both strategic and tactical, in reinsuring that the Chinese would not intervene massively in the Vietnam difficulties, was clearly being overlooked by the many whose opposition was due primarily to fear of massive Chinese intervention. By "reinsurance" I mean that the Chinese obviously had no itch to intervene anyway, one reason being that they knew, even if most Americans did not, that they had been bested in Korea even by conventional weapons alone.[10] Also, the Chinese were

---

mark in the above sentence by, among other things, pointing to references in the press that the bomb-carrying capacity of our B-52s operating from Guam against Vietnam had been stepped up to 30 tons each. The use of tactical nuclear weapons would certainly have made those and comparable operations vastly more efficient, without necessarily increasing risk to friendly civilians or armed forces. That is not to say, however, that stepping up even by orders of magnitude the efficiency of these particular operations would necessarily have made a critical difference in the progress of the war. On the other hand, the possibility that imaginative use of special types of nuclear weapons much earlier in the campaign might have gone far toward defeating the Viet Cong without the commitment of large numbers of American ground forces ought to be recognized, even if one accepts that under the political circumstances prevailing it would probably have been unwise policy.

[10] Our greatest error occurred at the time the Communists indicated in 1951 their interest in ending the conflict. We abruptly halted as a "good will gesture" the ongoing highly successful UN offensive that was, it should have been apparent, causing the Communist forces to seek the negotiations in the first place. This sudden halting of our military pressure naturally permitted the previously desperate enemy to recover, and relieved him of any need to come to terms. As a result the negotiations dragged on for two years, during which some 14,000 more Americans lost their lives in the fitful but static fighting, besides which we settled for terms much less favorable than we could otherwise have got. Much of the material on which I am basing these remarks comes from the unpublished work of a colleague, Dr. Herbert Goldhamer, who participated in the prisoner interrogation which re-

probably not at all disposed—in this case fortunately—to believe published official American remarks about anything, including our desire to avoid
use of nuclear weapons even against them.

It is a fairly safe prediction, however, that the
Vietnam experience will promote a basic rethink-
ing in the United States, both in and outside official
circles, of the doctrine of "containment" which has
ruled American foreign policy since the end of
World War II. That does not mean that the United
States is likely to retreat as far as the original author of the term, George F. Kennan, recently
confessed he had, in referring to himself as "in
many respects sort of a neo-isolationist."[11] But those
guiding the country will certainly have to consider
anew the whole framework of applicability of the
doctrine. Surely few could now disagree with Mr.
Kennan where he said that the degree of involvement of the United States in Vietnam at the time
of his testimony, while creating "a new situation"
which perforce dominated our military and diplo-

vealed the serious straits of the Chinese armies. For a report on
the relevant views, twelve years after the event, of Dean Acheson,
who had supported the recommendations to President Truman for
the stopping of the offensive and who still had no conception of
the strategic blunder it had entailed, see my contribution to the
symposium edited by Leland Hazard, *Empire Revisited* (Richard
D. Irwin, Inc., Homewood, Ill.), pp. 72f.

[11] See his comments before the Senate Foreign Relations Committee on February 10, 1966. The remark quoted here was not
part of Mr. Kennan's prepared statement, but was made in a
response to a question by Senator Case. Apart from the full
record published by the Committee, see either the *New York
Times* of February 11, 1966, or (for a fuller account) *The New
Republic* of February 26, 1966.

matic policies, was surely not one we would have chosen had we been able to realize in preceding months and years the lack of real cohesion in the governmental structure in South Vietnam.

As one "high United States authority" put it, the Saigon turmoil of April 1966 was a " 'classic example of the impotency of a great power overwhelmingly committed to a weak political base.' "[12] We may at times find ourselves obliged to support a government abroad which in our own domestic and thus usually inapplicable terms is not altogether admirable, like that of the late Syngman Rhee in 1950 Korea, but that is less embarrassing than to find ourselves behind a government of which it is mostly a courtesy to say that it governs, not to mention the question of the consent of the governed. Of the latter, the dominant fact was that they had had quite too much of a war in which the stakes for most of them were relatively marginal.

In any case, neither the events in Vietnam nor in Europe were causing us to dismantle our ICBMs. We even considered and openly discussed the erection of an anti-ballistic missile system. Presumably we had a policy and a strategy for the use even of these instrument; much thought, effort, and money were being spent on them, although our expectations of actually having to use them were obviously low.

Similarly, so far as NATO is concerned, there is

[12] *The Wall Street Journal,* April 12, 1966.

no doubt going to be a concerted effort on the part of all or at least most of the remaining fourteen nations to conserve and reconstruct it during what is hoped is the temporary withdrawal of France. To do so requires that there be some kind of military strategy for the defense of Europe.

The very suggestion of "strategy" implies the anticipation of severe crisis. As Herman Kahn has put it, when an engineer puts up a structure designed to last twenty years or so, "he does not ask, 'Will it stand up on a pleasant June day?' He asks how it performs under stress, under hurricane, earthquake, snow load, fire, flood, thieves, fools, and vandals."[13] One should add, however, that the warranted strength of the structure also depends on its purpose, on the anticipation of the *probability* of some of the catastrophes above mentioned during the use span envisioned, and in many cases on the choice between having a structure able to withstand the worst possible catastrophes and not having one at all. Few dwellings are built to withstand tornadoes, and few architects would suggest that they should be. All but a minute fraction of these structures last out their natural lives without suffering such visitations or various other of the catastrophes that Kahn mentions.

Of course, insofar as we are talking about defense alliances, the analogy should perhaps be with fortresses rather than dwellings, and fortresses

[13] *On Thermonuclear War*, Princeton University Press, Princeton, 1960, p. 138.

should be able to withstand shot. On the other hand, apart from individual differences in temperament and thinking, one of the striking changes in the climate of the times since Kahn published the above-quoted lines is that today more of us feel, I think justly, that we can really afford to risk living in houses that fully exploit the aesthetic values of glass rather than in medieval fortresses or in underground shelters. Oddly, the same bomb that caused the fears of the fifties to which Kahn was giving expression at the end of that decade has caused also the more relaxed attitude of the sixties; and it has not only been a matter of getting used to it, though that helped. Whether Mr. Kahn himself would agree with this view I do not know and rather doubt,[14] but the remarkable change, since the bomb appeared, in the prevailing climate of expectation concerning the probability of future catastrophe is a good part of what this book is about.

I should like finally in this introduction to make two further points, both somewhat technical.

First, I have been taxed by some of my colleagues with the reminder that I had in the past asserted in print that there was no essential difference between tactical and strategic nuclear weapons to war-

---

[14] In former times it would have been easy to check, but geographical separation does make a difference. Here I should mention Mr. Kahn's most recent work, *On Escalation: Metaphors and Scenarios*, Praeger, New York, 1965. This work, unfortunately, was published too late to be of assistance to me in writing the essay which follows, especially since the latter had to spend some time in going through clearance. Otherwise, I should have had more than one occasion to mention it.

rant the distinction in terminology. I must admit to having said so, and will justify my changed views partly by acknowledgment of past error and partly on the grounds that technology has indeed moved on to the point where there are already very marked distinctions and where there could be even sharper ones if we exploited more of the possibilties for specialized bombs. Even in the past one was justified in saying that any nuclear weapon set aside for possible tactical use could legitimately be called a "tactical" weapon. However, the great growth in types of nuclear weapons, by no means as fully exploited as the "state of the art" makes possible, has established a large family of weapons which are specifically intended for possible tactical use and would rarely if ever be considered for strategic use.

Another and much more important point of criticism is that I have put myself in the position of arguing for the use or threat of use, when appropriate, of specific types of weapons in a limited and essentially tightly controlled manner, even though existing arrangements may make it quite difficult or even impossible to exercise such control. The latter part of the statement is probably true, but I nevertheless consider this criticism irrelevant over the long term. If it follows from the acceptance of the arguments I present in this book that whatever tactical nuclear doctrine we have is obsolete and ought to be altered, it can and should be so altered. I see no reason why this should not be feasible. Rigidity in doctrine is an old story, but so is the necessity for resisting it.

If it is true that most studies of the tactical use of nuclear weapons emphasize large-scale use and neglect small-scale, controlled use—including controlled use of special weapons not presently stockpiled but known or considered to be technically feasible—this neglect should be corrected, and with some urgency. There is plenty of planning manpower available to do the job. As in so many other issues, it is not a question of available resources, but of how they are applied.

Certainly the "just another weapon" conception embodied in the studies which picture tactical nuclear weapons as simply a mighty enhancement of firepower must be rejected utterly. Wars may no doubt be shortened by expanding the havoc and concentrating it in time, but that is too great a price to pay for the abridgment of time. We are interested in this book in tactical nuclear weapons primarily as a deterrent and, if they fail in that function, as a de-escalating device. The latter interest obliges us to concentrate on the prevailing assumption that they are in fact the opposite.

I · *Escalatory Fears and the Effectiveness of Local Resistance*

In PRINCIPLE, general nuclear war between the Soviet Union and the United States can start either full-blown—which is to say by direct surprise attack by one side upon the other, either from a condition of peace or after just enough hostilities to activate the "tripwire"—or by escalation from lesser conflicts. Not long ago it was only the sudden surprise onset that was considered a real possibility. The need to strike *first* in a strategic exchange was too overwhelming to permit delay. In recent years, however, the conviction has spread and deepened that in the future, so long as we keep something like our present posture, general war can hardly occur except through escalation from lesser conflicts.

What has happened is that the constraints to refrain from strategic nuclear attack at *any* time, including a time of fairly intense local hostilities, have become great and also obvious, especially for the side that sees its opponent as having something like the superior strength which the Russians must view us as having.[1] The chief and almost the sole incentive for moving fast in such an attack in the past, which was to destroy the enemy's retaliatory force before it left the ground, has in the last

---

[1] The question of what *is* superior strength in a nuclear age will be treated later, pp. 31f., and 76f.

several years been sharply declining as a compelling operative constraint.

It is not essential to the analysis which is to follow to establish just how complete are our present and future guarantees against surprise strategic attack. However, it *is* relevant that the chances of such attack appear on the whole very small, and that the great reduction in our fears of it is based on good reasons and not on mere wishful thinking. The basic physical reason is the enormous and continuing improvement in the security of our retaliatory forces (and presumably also the enemy's) against attack through the well-known devices of hardening, concealment, and mobility. This improvement may indeed be threatened in the future by certain technological advances, but it need not be overturned if we remain fully abreast of ongoing developments.

Our confidence is further increased by the fact that this physical change has served to buttress a comparably profound psychological change. The latter results from a greatly improved understanding, apparently on the Soviet Russian side as well as our own, of the motivations and psychology of the opponent. The reasons for this improvement in mutual insight are many, but the essential fact is that each side seems to have scaled down substantially the degree of aggressiveness, recklessness, or callousness it formerly attributed to the other—also both have now grown accustomed to living with each other under a situation that once seemed intolerably menacing. Stability does not thrive on illusion, but it does help enormously to have the situation turn other than precarious.

This basic change in the world's political and strategic environment, which has taken place mostly during the last decade and which was both demonstrated and advanced by the outcome of the Cuban missile crisis of 1962,[2] is no doubt in the net a considerable gain for everybody. It is not without its price—some would argue a serious price. Although the threat of massive retaliation has long been discounted by strategic analysts as being inappropriate for coping with relatively small-scale aggressions or infractions by the opponent, it did seem not so long ago to be a valid means of dealing with possible aggressions that might be deliberate and massive though still local, either in Europe or in Asia.

The famous speech by the late John Foster Dulles of January 12, 1954, in which he did not invent but merely reasserted the threat of retaliating "massively," was largely a warning to the Chinese not to risk a resumption of the Korean War. As such, it was not at all unbelievable. Moreover, almost no one at that time doubted—surely the Rus-

[2] Whatever else we may say about that crisis, it is clear from its outcome that the Russians never thought they were actually risking war by putting the missiles into Cuba. Certainly they removed them with alacrity as soon as President Kennedy made clear his readiness to back his warnings with use of force, and in doing so they took no pains at all to hide their great aversion to *any* hostilities with us, however limited. See A. L. Horelick, "The Cuban Missile Crisis: An Analysis of Soviet Calculations and Behavior," *World Politics*, xvi (April 1964), 363-389.

sians did not doubt—that a deliberate Soviet attack against Western Europe (which everyone took for granted would inevitably be massive) would be met with an immediate American strategic nuclear attack against the Soviet Union.

The time for insisting mainly on such strategies, or rather threats, is clearly past. Whether or not credibility would have survived for some time longer in the world outside if we had continued to insist upon it as the strategy to which we were wholeheartedly committed is no longer at issue. The dominant fact is that U. S. official pronouncements have for some time been committing us to the principle that local aggressions on the part of our major opponents must at least initially be resisted locally. The possibility of further escalation will, to be sure, be unavoidably but also usefully present. It will tend to induce caution on both sides, but it will more especially tend to dissuade the aggressor from testing very far the efficacy of a *resolute* local defense.[3]

In short, vis-à-vis the Soviet Union we can no longer effectively threaten general war as *an initial response* to anything other than a direct strategic attack upon us. However, our strategic nuclear capabilities cannot fail to play an important role in any serious crisis. What we can and no doubt will threaten in such an instance will be some move or action which, so long as it spells violence, *could*

---

[3] The asymmetry suggested here between attacker and defender will be clarified in Chapter 6; see especially pp. 81-84. It does *not* depend on any assumed tactical advantage for the defender.

escalate. We have to leave to the opponent in his next move the choice of making the situation more dangerous or less so, though we can of course massively influence the choice he will make.

The present relevance of all this is partly that in the strategic dialogue that is always proceeding within NATO, publicly and otherwise, we are in some danger of missing the special character of certain recent European complaints. One of our replies to the alarm which some of our allies have expressed over our earlier preoccupation with conventional forces has taken the form of stressing the rapid growth of our store of tactical nuclear weapons in Europe, coupled with renewed affirmation that they would be used if necessary. From the French especially the response has been that our willingness to use *tactical* nuclear weapons does not reassure them. The French premier, Georges Pompidou, echoing President de Gaulle, has declared that such use would make Europe the scorched battleground and leave the United States untouched. This is not a new argument, to be sure, but we had rather lost sight of it. Worse still, the people who think this way *equate American unwillingness to initiate and thus undergo strategic bombing with an unwillingness or an inability to defend them.* Our open national response to such charges has been in general to express shock that our intentions and good faith have been questioned, and then to fall back on ambiguities concerning those intentions.

Where Europeans insist that we will surely be

unwilling to hazard national extermination for them, it is useless to try to persuade them that we will indeed be ready to do so. We should rather emphasize the fact—which is to their decided advantage—that there is no need for us to initiate (and thus to undergo) strategic bombing in order to defend them effectively. The threat of an effective local defense—which is to say one that is serious enough either to succeed in itself or to open up the possibilities for larger scale action—is a deterrent as good as or better than any threat of general war, especially since it is far less subject to being doubted.

We could remind the French that in 1917 and again in 1941 our European allies did not resent or reject our military support of them on the ground that we could not for obvious geographical reasons fully share their anguish and their vital danger. History and geography had put the enemy on their borders, not on ours. The idea that Europe can and should be defended in Europe, at least to begin with, can hardly be bizarre, novel, or abhorrent to the Europeans—provided it is confronted honestly.[4] Naturally the Europeans don't want to be the battleground for our own quarrels with the Russians, but that means only that our main job of persuasion is to convince the Europeans that we

---

[4] It should be noted in passing that it is not this aspect of NATO that De Gaulle finds mainly objectionable. His preferences seem to be for a looser alliance than the present one, presumably because he finds the American influence in the present one too overbearing. Obviously, one major reason he can indulge that feeling is that he entertains a low estimate of the current or near future need for our military assistance.

will never fight the Russians in Europe except in the direct defense of Europe. This might mean, among other things, an appropriate revision of Article 5 of the North Atlantic Treaty, which equated North America with Europe as an area in which enemy attack might be initiated. And it cannot be too often repeated that for the Europeans, as indeed also for us, the main purpose of *any* kind of nuclear threat, however local, is deterrence.

Anyway, to return to our main theme: when looked at whole, the situation today is without doubt enormously preferable to that which faced us formerly. Then we not only had to be prepared against surprise attack—we still do, in order to keep its probability low—but also feared it as something which, we thought, had a much more than trivial chance of happening in our lifetime.

The present situation is often spoken of as the "nuclear stalemate." It is a valid enough characterization if we are clear that it does not make superiority meaningless, and provided we remember that the "stalemate" applies properly only to a *strategic* exchange between the United States and the Soviet Union. The latter point has to be stressed because the term is often indiscriminately applied, especially by laymen, to any use of nuclear weapons. An argument we shall have occasion to develop later is that the existence of a nuclear stalemate on the strategic level may indeed favor rather than prohibit the use of nuclear weapons on the tactical level.

The superiority referred to above can be found

meaningful according to a number of criteria, but probably the most important is that it interposes a significant and obvious differential between the opponents in the military reasonableness of their being willing to take any of the successive steps in the escalatory process. There are many differences, not only in numbers but also in technological aspects of weapons performance, which do not meet the public eye but which are regarded by professionals as important—perhaps with some exaggeration at times, but by no means always so. A simpler way of dealing with the question would be to ask whether the Soviet Union would willingly exchange nuclear postures with us (including tactical nuclear weapons), and the answer seems to be at least suggested in the fact that they have paid a much higher and more painful proportion of their much more limited resources for what they have than we have for ours. In economists' terms, the "marginal utility" of the last piece of nuclear weaponry they have bought must seem to them to be pretty high, and they clearly possess a good deal less of it than we do.

The very easement of the danger of surprise strategic attack has stimulated a special fear of what in quite recent times has come to be called escalation. The fact that it seems to be the only way, or at any rate much the least unlikely way, in which general war can occur helps to focus attention on it. Previously one took for granted—as the Soviet political and military leaders apparently

still do—that any outbreak of unambiguous hostilities between the Soviet Union and the United
States would escalate almost immediately to general
war. We therefore concentrated our concern on
avoiding the outbreak of war, rather than on the
escalation that we feared must surely follow such
an outbreak. However, as soon as people sensed
the possibility that we could have a war even with
the Soviet Union that might stay limited, then
escalation, which is to say the erosion or collapse
of limitations, became quite appropriately the object of special attention. It was natural, even if not
altogether logical, that concentration on avoiding
escalation should tend among specialists to displace
in importance the object of avoiding the outbreak
of war.

We must be prepared also for a somewhat comparable displacement of attention with respect to
the tactical use of nuclear weapons. It was not until sophisticated persons began to discern the possibility, through restraint in fighting, of avoiding
the worst imaginable kind of holocaust, which is to
say unlimited war, that the abhorrence that most
civilized people feel towards nuclear weapons
tended to be focused on the *tactical* use of such
weapons in limited war. The intense desire to avoid
any use of nuclear weapons quite naturally provoked the allegation that use of them in limited
war would be critical in tripping off uncontrolled
escalation.

It is worth recording that the process here de-

scribed took considerable time. Ideas concerning
modern limited war had been bruited about in the
United States for some years, and were greeted with
skepticism enough, before the additionally novel
thought began to be suggested that limited wars,
even fairly large ones, could and ought to be fought
by conventional means alone. Thus, those relevant
ideas that seem to many today to be utterly self-
evident were manifestly not so to most strategic
thinkers in the middle and late fifties. (See above,
pp. 4-6).

It may be most desirable for *other reasons,* especially political reasons, to avoid any use of nuclear
weapons, and it may even be true that resort to
such weapons could be the critical factor in provoking uncontrolled escalation (obviously, introduction of nuclear weapons is itself an important kind
of escalation); but the two points are distinct, and
evidence to support the latter contention does not
flow automatically from those other reasons. The
reverse may in fact be the case; a weapon which is
feared and abhorred is so much the less likely to be
used *automatically* in response to any kind of signal, including even the enemy's use of it.

It is, however, obvious that views attributing a
powerful and automatic escalatory stimulus to nuclear weapons—views not the less firmly advanced
for being based entirely on intuition—have been
of critical importance in molding attitudes toward
appropriate strategies in the event of limited war,
especially in any conflict between the United States

and the Soviet Union or China. These views have thereby greatly affected force postures, recommended and realized, for ourselves and for our allies. The ramifications of these attitudes, and the disagreements they engender, affect the whole gamut of national defense policies.

II · The Analytical Problem

WE SHOULD make clear that there appear to be no special tools, devices, or gimmicks by which we may drastically improve our predictions concerning the chances of escalation in any crisis. There seems to be no substitute for old-fashioned analysis, applied with special discipline to the problem that concerns us. We are looking for relevant generalizations in which we can have high confidence and which will importantly assist us to estimate the risks of escalation in the event of any confrontation between the United States and either of our major opponents, especially over the near term (that is, about ten years). We specify the near term because over the longer term conditions tend to change basically, and, insofar as new analysis is needed, the future can take care of itself.

In this pursuit we are dealing with issues of human behavior under great emotional stress in circumstances that have never been experienced. We will find standing in our way some operationally entrenched generalizations based on intuited assumptions on which widespread consensus exists but which have rarely if ever been critically examined. Use of techniques like war gaming or crisis gaming helps to enlarge the perspectives of the players and to make them more comprehensive in their thinking, but it provides neither them nor those who read their reports with answers to the

crucial questions. Experienced persons agree that
one simply cannot reproduce among the players in
a gaming environment the kind and degree of emotional tension and feeling of high responsibility
bound to be present in the nuclear era among deci-
sion-makers in real-life crises, where decisions have
to be made about whether and by what means to
fight a war. In games, erroneous moves are free of
penalties of the required magnitude; the appropriate degree of fear or dread on both sides is thus
only dimly imagined, and feelings of anger or hostility may be exaggerated in importance.

That does not mean that players always act more
boldly in gaming various imagined crises than the
same persons might in comparable decision-making
positions in a real crisis;[1] it means only that their
reasons for acting either timidly or boldly have almost always been formed independently of the
game environment. The players are usually ex-
pressing by their moves their respective conceptions
or understanding of how leaders in the real world
operate under comparable situations, for example,
their conceptions of when considerations of prestige dominate over fear, or vice versa. The degree
of political and psychological sophistication represented in the process may be considerable or it
may not, and whether it is or not is certainly more

[1] One of the important constraints in gaming is the desire to
avoid appearing wildly illogical in the eyes of one's colleagues.
Such constraints, while providing useful discipline, obviously
depend on the correctness of the consensus on what constitutes
"wildly illogical behavior." In trying to clear away ancient error,
consensus is always our greatest enemy.

important than the elegance or complexity of the game.

Certainly this is no criticism of gaming. In many kinds of inquiries we cannot really cope with our problems by any other means.[2] We suggest only that for many purposes the improvement of the players' conceptions and understandings of the world they live in is much more essential to our ends than the use of the game technique itself, which can, however, become usefully supplemental.

We shall have to consider first in some breadth and depth the more important factors bearing upon the relevant decisions that national leaders will make in anticipation of an outbreak of fighting, and, if the outbreak occurs, during the early stages of such fighting. We shall try to imagine various crisis situations from which one could conceive hostilities breaking out, asking at each critical point in the imagined sequence of events (thus preserving something of the game technique) what would be the likely constraints upon each side and the various options open to each or, rather, how at the time would they be likely to appear to each side. What are likely to be the emotions as well as the strategic and political considerations guiding the responsible leaders, and how are those emotions

[2] See my comments on the uses and limitations of gaming in my *Strategy in the Missile Age,* Princeton University Press, Princeton, 1959, pp. 246-247, 385-389. Unfortunately, some of my former RAND colleagues who have written valuable papers on the subject have not seen fit to publish them, for reasons not connected with security. Outstanding among these authors is William Jones.

likely to affect their perception of the situation?

We shall thereby be attempting to clarify just how and by what steps local and limited war *could* develop into a general war. We shall also be asking and attempting to answer questions like the following: What conditions would, in general, favor unwanted escalation? What would cause the existence of such conditions? What could we prudently do in advance to modify or eliminate them?

In this exercise we shall have to bring intimately into play our knowledge of our two major Communist opponents, especially the Soviet Union. That knowledge is today, among the appropriate experts, quite considerable, being based on continuing intensive analysis of a very large body of data, including that derived from our own fairly prolonged, crisis-laden national experience with the Russians. Concerning the Chinese, about whom we have less knowledge but still a significant and most useful amount, it would seem to be obvious that in any fighting with them over the next ten years we really ought not to have to worry overmuch about escalation that reached or threatened to reach the use of nuclear weapons—unless, as is most unlikely, the Soviet Union supported them to the hilt—because their nuclear capabilities, either tactical or strategic, will obviously bear no comparison to ours.

We could, to be sure, allow ourselves to be paralyzed by anxiety about what the Chinese could do with just a few bombs and delivery vehicles, for example, bomb Tokyo, or even some half dozen American cities. It is something to consider, but not, it is to be hoped, through forsaking entirely any reasonable perspective. Our government seemed to find it easy to write off the French nuclear effort (especially when considered independently) as relatively useless, and the French effort will be for some time by orders of magnitude more impressive than the Chinese.

Most amazing, in my opinion, is the recently developed argument that a junior-grade anti-ballistic-missile defense which would be insufficient to do any good against a Soviet strategic attack should nevertheless be provided in the United States against Chinese strategic attack. Curiously, some of the originators and promoters of this idea were prominent in ridiculing as ineffective the French nuclear effort.[3]

[3] For a good reply to this argument, mostly on technical grounds, see J. I. Coffey, "The Chinese and Ballistic Missile Defense," *Bulletin of the Atomic Scientists*, xxi (December 1965), 17-20.

III · *The Relevant Image of the Opponent*

IT IS necessary now to mention some relevant facts about our opponents, especially the Soviet leaders. Estimating probabilities of escalation is essentially an exercise in predicting the behavior of those leaders (as well as our own) under various kinds of crisis situations. The areas of uncertainty may be broad enough, but we are not dealing with mysterious and unknown elements. There is, among other things, a copious record that can usefully be studied.

The first point to notice is that the political leaders of the Soviet Union appear today to believe quite as deeply as our own in the utterly catastrophic nature of general nuclear war. If there are any differences between the two governments in respective degrees of conviction, these differences are certainly too marginal to be politically significant. Besides, by whatever standards of measurement one chooses to adopt, the American strength in retaliatory power is, for the present and near future at least, enormously greater than that of the Soviet Union, and they are fully aware of this difference. Certainly too we have the resource capability to retain this advantage for as long as we are determined to.

Soviet feelings about nuclear war are abundantly manifest in Soviet utterances as well as behavior, including their contributions to the bitter dialogue between Peking and Moscow. And incidentally, when Moscow charged Peking with not being sufficiently aware of the terrible hazards of general nuclear war, Peking replied not by challenging the Soviet view but by denying that it had been insensitive to those hazards![1]

In a speech in Hungary during the spring of 1964, the Soviet premier, Khrushchev, remarked: "Only a child or an idiot does not fear war." Later, on signing the "friendship pact" with the East Germans in June 1964, he declared: "Nuclear war is stupid, stupid, stupid! If you reach for the push button you reach for suicide." These remarks prove nothing in themselves, but they do reflect, what is confirmed from other indices, a quite different world from that existing before 1939, let alone before 1914. Nor is there any indication that Khrushchev's successors, Brezhnev and Kosygin, differ significantly from him in these respects.

The second point is that when the record of the Soviet Union since the end of World War II is examined carefully, there emerges an image of a government that combines in a quite unprecedented manner (a) political aggressiveness and an itch for probing with (b) extreme military caution. The Russians have been most respectful of our

[1] See the "Chinese Government Statement" of 1 September 1963, reprinted in English translation in *Survival*, v (November-December 1963), 263-268. See also Alice Langley Hsieh, "The Sino-Soviet Nuclear Dialogue: 1963," *The Journal of Conflict Resolution*, June 1964, and also reprinted in *Survival*, vi (September-October 1964), 228-239.

strength, and prudent. That does not in itself mean that they cannot change in the future and become militarily aggressive, but we should be clear that it would have to be a change, and a profound one. Moreover, since the Cuban crisis of October 1962 the trends seem to have been entirely in the opposite direction.

The evidence for the above statements is quickly outlined. Perhaps the most conspicuous instance since World War II of what we usually think of as Soviet aggressiveness was the so-called Berlin blockade of 1948-49. In retrospect it is difficult to find evidence of any threat of force by the Soviet leaders to deny us ground access to Berlin. On the contrary, the measures that finally induced us to resort to the airlift at the end of June 1948 were instituted gradually over a three-month period—though the most serious of them were concentrated in the final two weeks. We may be sure that each measure was imposed tentatively for the purpose of observing our response.[2] As General Lucius D. Clay later wrote:

> The care with which the Russians avoided measures which would have been resisted with force had convinced me that the Soviet Government

[2] See Jean Edward Smith, *The Defense of Berlin*, Johns Hopkins Press, Baltimore, 1963, pp. 103-130; also Philip Windsor, *City on Leave*, London, 1963, pp. 98-126. Neither author makes the points I am making here, but they provide data for them. See also W. Phillips Davison, *The Berlin Blockade: A Study in Cold War Politics*, Princeton University Press, Princeton, 1958, especially pp. 98ff.

did not want war although it believed that the Western Allies would yield much of their position rather than risk war. . . . I reported this conviction . . . suggesting that we advise the Soviet representatives in Germany that under our rights to be in Berlin we proposed on a specific date to move an armed convoy which would be equipped with the engineering material to overcome the technical difficulties which the Soviet representatives appeared unable to solve. . . .

In my view the chances of such a convoy being met by force with subsequent developments of hostilities were small. I was confident that it would get through to Berlin and that the highway blockade would be ended. . . .[3]

What is perhaps most telling is that even after we had underlined our own pacific intentions (or

[3] From his *Decision in Germany*, New York, 1950, p. 375, quoted in Smith, *op. cit.*, p. 117. Robert Murphy, in his memoirs published *Diplomat Among Warriors*, New York, 1964, has indicated that he thought of resigning over the issue of our accepting the presumed denial of access on the ground, and he now regrets that he did not do so; see pp. 313-323. The Mayor of West Berlin, Ernst Reuter, an ex-Communist who knew the Russians well, was convinced that the Soviets were bluffing and that they would lift the "blockade" immediately if an armored column pushed up the highway from Helmstedt. Among others who had the same conviction was the left-wing British Labour Party leader, Aneurin Bevan. On the basis of our present knowledge, it appears practically certain that the appraisal shared by Clay, Murphy, Reuter, and Bevan was correct. Such a conclusion, however, does not seriously impugn the judgment of those who thought otherwise at the time; we are after all now speaking with the benefit of considerable hindsight, and the costs of a wrong judgment appeared then to be pretty high.

anxieties) by accepting the presumed denial of ground access, the Russians made not the slightest attempt to interfere with our only alternative means of access, the airlift, as they could easily have done, for example, by jamming our ground-controlled-approach radar. Because of the many days of marginal flying conditions in Berlin, especially through the long winter, such jamming would have interfered seriously with the success of the airlift. This hardly suggests the temper of a blockade. No doubt the Russians desired us to interpret their actions as a blockade, but only so long as we were not ready to test our interpretation with force.

The two Berlin "crises" of 1958 and 1961 were brought about in each case simply by a Russian threat, with a declared deadline, to sign a separate peace treaty with the East Germans. Though we were obliged to regard such a threat seriously because of certain implications, in neither crisis was there any direct threat of their using force to deny us access. In each case, moreover, the deadline was allowed to drift by without the threatened action. No doubt the vigor of our response was responsible for the Soviet backtracking. But it is certainly questionable whether our response in the latter case needed to go as far as calling up large numbers of reserves and substantially reinforcing our air forces in Europe.

Finally we come to the Cuban crisis of October 1962. The fact that the Russians put offensive missiles and bombers into Cuba has often since been urged as proof of both their unpredictability and their aggressiveness. It is no doubt a salutary reminder that specific expectations may go awry. However, in estimating the degree of Soviet aggressiveness reflected in the move, one cannot permit any arbitrary divorcement of that phase of the operation from the concluding phase. The same leader responsible for putting the missiles in took them out again, hastily and even ignominiously, when he saw that the United States was ready to back up with force its demands for their removal. The circumstances of that removal must surely qualify one's estimate of his boldness in putting the missiles in. Khrushchev may have been foolish, but was he really being foolhardy? Clearly he not only did not want war, but he thought he was taking no real risk of it.

A question often asked after the event and as often speculatively answered was: What was the Soviet purpose in putting in the missiles? Rarely asked but more urgent for future guidance is the question: What did *we* do to make them think we would let them get away with it? Obviously, their thinking so was critical to the whole operation. Our behavior in the Bay of Pigs episode and thereafter apparently led the Russians to expect that, despite our words to the contrary, we would accept the missiles and bombers in Cuba as we had accepted the earlier phases of their military buildup.

One Soviet expectation was indeed fulfilled—that if they had to retreat they would be permitted to do so, that is, that upon discovery of the missiles in Cuba we would not initiate hostilities without further warning. This expectation being both reasonable and, as it turned out, correct, the actual risks they were taking appeared to them certainly manageable. Even if we had attacked their Cuban missile bases without further warning, which they clearly did not expect, they had control of their response, and they had no obligation or intention to commit suicide. Can one say, then, that our previous knowledge of the Russians, accumulated over a whole generation of intense study, was put to naught? Deepened that knowledge certainly was, but the key lessons concerned our own errors. We should not have let them think they could get away with it. Our having made a bad prediction does not itself justify our calling the Russians "unpredictable."

Another extremely significant aspect of that crisis is that Soviet behavior during it and afterward was conspicuously more cooperative also concerning Berlin. This behavior ran directly contrary to the expectations of our own and allied leaders following President Kennedy's October 22 speech.[4] Certainly this demonstration, unique in the postwar world, of our readiness to use force directly against

---

[4] One British Foreign Office official informed this writer that when the President's speech was heard in the United Kingdom, "the Foreign Office, to a man, expected the Russians to be in West Berlin on the following day." It is worthwhile considering why they were so wrong. Unfortunately, making post mortems on bad guesses does not appear to be a popular activity in any government.

Soviet-manned installations, and to oppose an action that did not even involve a violation of frontiers, must have come as a great shock to the Soviet leaders. Obviously it was a salutary one, as subsequent events amply demonstrated. No doubt confirming the salutariness of the lesson were the later revelations by T. C. Sorenson and others that members of our government had for a time actually considered making a surprise attack on those bases.[5]

The above episodes largely sum up the record, overwhelmingly negative, of Soviet military initiative along the whole of that long line of demarcation on which the NATO Powers have confronted the Soviet power since the end of World War II. In those twenty years there has been no infringement of frontiers and not the slightest skirmish between their troops and ours. Some of our planes have fallen to their fire, but always under circumstances where the Russians could at least claim we were overflying their territory. Besides, the record established long ago that such attacks do not bring reprisals. Contrary to U.S. expectations of ten years ago or more, the Russians have shown themselves relatively careful to avoid making unauthorized flights over our territories.[6]

[5] See Theodore C. Sorenson, *Kennedy*, Harper and Row, New York, 1965, pp. 682-685.

[6] One early objection to the DEW (Distant Early Warning) line across central Canada was that the Russians could and would spoof it to death. So far as is publicly known, they have not attempted to spoof it at all. They have, of course, behaved very differently with U.S. Navy ships at sea, taking full and often annoying advantage, with both air and surface craft, of the fact that legally the sea is an international common.

It is against this record that we must consider the "scenarios" (that is, examinations of imaginary attacks and ensuing battles) often produced in support of American pleas of the early sixties for substantially building up NATO conventional forces in Europe. That an image of the Soviet Union which grossly inflated Soviet military aggressiveness should be used to justify the need for more *conventional* forces is paradoxical, but we have gotten used to the paradox. Anyway, the contrary image of a Soviet Union that had been completely deterred from aggressive military action by something like our existing military posture at home and in Europe hardly presented a good case for the costly conventional buildup we were urging. The two premises necessary to justify that buildup were thus (a) Soviet alleged military aggressiveness, expressed in (b) imputed readiness *to assault our nuclear-armed forces with conventional arms alone.* Such conduct would be both unprecedented and fantastically "adventuristic," a trait to which Russian Communism has long been known to be peculiarly inhospitable.

One distinguished writer has indeed remarked that "the record was replete with instances" where nuclear deterrence had failed in Europe, but the only specific example he gives was the building of "the monstrous Wall dividing East Berlin from West Berlin," which began to go up on August 13, 1961.[7] But, apart from the fact that the Wall was

[7] William W. Kaufmann, *The McNamara Strategy*, Harper and

placed on Soviet-held territory, one might well ask: What would we have been prepared to do about it if we had ten more conventional divisions in Europe, or twenty? Contrarily, if we wanted to do something bold, why did it require a single additional soldier? In other words, how much did the strictly local forces affect the Russians' willingness or unwillingness to risk open hostilities with us—or, for that matter, our willingness or unwillingness to get into such hostilities with them?

Actually, the greatest single challenge to the status quo, the greatest "failure of deterrence"— though we must avoid confusing an occasionally necessary confrontation with failure of deterrence —was precisely the Cuban crisis of October 1962, when our conventional forces had already been very considerably built up by the Kennedy administration. After the event various persons attributed Khrushchev's spectacular retreat primarily to our large conventional superiority in the Caribbean. But, somewhat oddly, Defense Secretary Robert S. McNamara expressed himself before a congressional committee as thinking otherwise. Among his words were: ". . . in any event Khrushchev knew without any question whatsoever that he faced the full military power of the United States, including its nuclear weapons . . . and that is the reason, and the only reason, why he withdrew those weapons."[8]

Row, New York, 1964, especially pp. 72, 106, 118f., 128, and 258. See also my review article on this book, "The McNamara Phenomenon," *World Politics*, XVII (July 1965), 672-686.

[8] *Department of Defense Appropriations for 1964*, Part I, Hearings before a Subcommittee on Appropriations, House of Representatives, 88th Congress, 1st Session, 1963, pp. 30-31.

However, there has been a shift in emphasis in recent years to the possibility of "accidental" war. The various concepts of accidental war tend to have in common a condition, following some initiating event, in which both sides find themselves engaged in hostilities which neither side wants—in fact which both sides may have been desperately anxious to avoid. The variety of ways in which such a circumstance is supposed to come about include mainly (a) "miscalculation," usually in the form of a probing action by the Soviet Union which has escalated but which was originally prompted by the erroneous assumption that the West would not resist at all, or would make only token resistance, or (b) some "unauthorized actions" by the military personnel of one side against the other which lead to (perhaps also unauthorized) local retaliation.

It is actually quite difficult to find historical examples of "accidental war" which fit easily either of these patterns. Political leaders have sometimes underestimated the resolve of a potential opponent to react staunchly against some planned aggressive action, as Hitler underestimated in 1939 the finally achieved resolve of the British and French governments to go to war with him because of his conquest of Poland, or as General Douglas MacArthur and the Truman administration underestimated the readiness of the Communist Chinese to intervene in the Korean War as the UN forces approached the Yalu. No doubt also the original North Korean attack was launched in the confident expectation that the fairly concrete words of certain American leaders, like Secretary of State Dean Acheson, meant that the United States would not intervene.[9]

However, the actions that elicited these unexpected responses were a good deal more than "probing actions," a term which implies the opportunity and capacity to withdraw the probe. Though in each case mentioned there was certainly some degree of "miscalculation," it would be stretching the term considerably to call any of the ensuing wars "accidental." Hitler would unquestionably have invaded Poland anyway—the British and French governments did do their best to make their commitment clear—and in other examples cited the party launching the aggression was clearly willing to accept substantial risks. Despite the unexpected Chinese intervention (unexpected especially by General Douglas MacArthur, who often demonstrated, usually with more brilliant results, his capacity for playing hunches), the most surprising thing about the Korean War—something that would not have been predicted at all before the event—was the degree to which escalation was in fact controlled and stopped.

So far as concerns the statesmen's perennial nightmare of "unauthorized action" by military personnel, one has to observe that military officers

[9] The reference is to the famous "Perimeter Speech" of Secretary Acheson before the National Press Club, Washington, on January 12, 1950, reprinted in *Department of State Bulletin*, January 23, 1950.

are intensively trained above all to obey the orders
of legally authorized superiors, especially in the
kind of established and well-ordered states that we
are usually thinking of when we talk of the possibility of nuclear war among the powers. Revolts
like that of the four French generals in Algeria in
the spring of 1961, which incidentally did not involve an attack on another power, are exceedingly
rare in the history of France or of other European
countries. In this instance the circumstances were
of a very special nature; even so, the revolt quickly
collapsed because of the unwillingness of the great
majority of French officers in Algeria to counte-
nance mutiny and, for that matter, because of the
basically nonmutinous dispositions of the chief
actors themselves.

So far as the American and the Soviet military
forces are concerned, the tradition in each case
of complete and dedicated subordination by the
military to civilian authority reveals hardly any
impairment historically. The insubordination that
President Truman charged against General Mac-
Arthur concerned activity of a political rather
than a military nature, involving mainly unauthorized letters and statements to the press, and
no one challenged the President's authority to re-
move the prestigious MacArthur. Historically it is
no problem to find many instances of conspicuous
restraint on the part of the military, and very difficult to find the reverse. One thinks of General
Beauregard wiring the confederate capital in Mont-

gomery for a reconfirmation of his orders before opening fire on Fort Sumter, or, on the British side, Admiral Milne in the Mediterranean tracking the *Breslau* and the *Goeben* on August 4, 1914, waiting for his government's ultimatum to expire at midnight before opening fire—thereby losing his chance altogether.

We also know enough in detail about the Soviet armed forces since the Revolution to have more than the usual confidence that the Soviet military leaders are accustomed to obeying the leaders of the party and the government. The services which permitted thousands of their officers, including those of the very highest rank, to be murdered by Stalin in the purge of the late thirties without the slightest move of opposition, and which in war and peace have tolerated a degree of intrusion by the "political commissar" that a Western officer would consider simply unthinkable, have, to put it mildly, a tradition of obedience.

It has sometimes been alleged since the Cuban crisis of October 1962 that the senior officers of the Soviet armed forces "resented" Khrushchev's pusillanimous retreat. Quite possibly they did, but evidence that they were ready to do anything about it, or that they played any part at all in the fall of Khrushchev two years later, seems to be entirely lacking.[10]

---

[10] I would naturally refrain from making such observations in an area where I have no personal expertise were I not supported in my views by colleagues who do have the requisite expertise in abundance, especially Drs. Roman Kolkowicz and Thomas W. Wolfe.

What should now cause accidental war of either variety described above to become more probable in a nuclear age than it has been in the past? We hear mention of the possibility of gadgetry malfunctioning, but fear of such possibilities has already, certainly on our side and presumably on the other as well, caused extensive and elaborate precautionary measures to be taken. The military, for their part, have been placed under tighter restrictions than ever before, as evidenced by the revelation (in press reports for July 15, 1964) that an American officer who was slapped by an East Berlin guard was under orders, which he obeyed, not to strike back.

However, even if one can imagine opposing military units breaking into combat with each other against the wishes of their governments, *one must also explain how and why such hostilities should grow swiftly to large dimensions.* The scenario which depicts this kind of happening usually has to impute to both sides (a) a well-nigh limitless concern with saving face, regardless of risks, and/ or (b) a great deal of ground-in automaticity of response and counterresponse, resulting in a swiftly accelerating ascent in scale of violence. There are bound to exist tendencies in these directions, which perhaps needs to be watched carefully. But these tendencies do not exist in a vacuum. We should not forget, among other things, that governments maintain communications with their officers in the field, and governments are rarely unmindful of risks.

Of late a good deal of emphasis has been put on

still another kind of "accidental" or at least "un-premeditated" war—that which begins with an up-rising in a Communist-ruled country contiguous with the West, followed by a more or less irrepressible intervention from our side. The place most often mentioned is East Germany, and it is easy to conjure up a picture of West German troops streaming across the border to help their brethren. This would of course be another form of "unauthorized" military action, which we have already considered, though one also can imagine some degree of complicity on the part of the government of the Federal Republic. If so, it would have to be in an atmosphere different from the present one.

To be sure, in theory the "accidental" war might arise from an initiative on our part, such as has been advocated by Dean Acheson. In a series of public statements he has urged that we and especially our allies proceed with a large conventional buildup in order deliberately to force the Russians out of East Germany, presumably through the exploitation or even the stimulation of an uprising. This would bring about the unification of Germany without which, according to Mr. Acheson, peace in Europe cannot ultimately be preserved.[11]

[11] One such speech by Mr. Acheson was delivered on September 30, 1963, at the Fifth Annual Conference, in Cambridge, England, of the Institute for Strategic Studies. This speech is published in No. 5 of the "Adelphi Papers" issued by the Institute, bearing the title "The Evolution of NATO." Repeated throughout much of Europe during that autumn, variations of this speech by Mr. Acheson provoked strongly negative responses from his audiences (as this writer had occasion in two instances to witness).

In this appeal, Mr. Acheson seems not to have any following. Even those Germans who might share his views on the importance of Germany's reunification are unlikely to consider the preservation of peace in the future a good reason for breaking that peace now. Other Europeans are even more ready to take their chances with a postponement of reunification.

It would be foolish and irresponsible to insist that accidental war is impossible or that the efforts to picture its occurrence in scenarios are misguided. On the contrary, insofar as we are interested in this book primarily in appraising the factors bearing on escalation, we may have to posit or presume hostilities breaking out accidentally in order to have a meaningful point of departure. However, if a conflict breaks out accidentally, *that fact itself would have to be of large and direct relevance to the estimates we must subsequently make about the chances of escalation.* But we cannot avoid bringing to bear on those estimates a searching inquiry of what the probabilities are for one type of action or reaction as compared with another.

No doubt the capability for dreaming up "far out" events is to be cultivated and cherished, but so is the capability for applying a disciplined judgment about the probability of those events. To do otherwise, to insist always on acting as though the worst conceivable outcome has as good a chance as any of coming to pass, is—especially on the issue of escalation—not "playing it safe" but rather needlessly giving away all one's advantages to the opponent.

The same is true of the element of change, which is indeed inevitable—change in the character of governments and in political conditions as well as in technology. But have we no clues about the changes the future will bring? Is it not also useful to remind ourselves that the governments of nations that are important to us tend to have distinctive characteristics that are expressed over long periods of time in fairly consistent modes of conduct? Deflections from normal conduct created by the accession to power of highly unusual individuals (for example, De Gaulle) can also be studied and weighed, and usually it is possible to make meaningful predictions about how long they will be around and what happens when they go. In short, although we are dealing always with uncertainties about the future, we are dealing also with governments having qualities that make them, in terms of what can be expected of them, akin to persons of known character. One should expect that absorbing the relevant empirical knowledge would therefore help us importantly with our predictions of the future—as expressed for example, in determining which war game scenarios or other types of implied models are relatively realistic, and which are not.

To be sure, important things happen that few had previously thought probable—*occasionally* things that no one had conceived of. That does not, however, establish that we must consequently abandon the notion that some things are very much more probable than others, and that with appropriate study we can have a good deal to say about which is which.[12] A good part of our uncertainty about the future is attributable to the fact that we do not know which contingency will in fact happen among the several that presently strike us as having a fairly good or at least more than an infinitesimal chance of happening. There are, on the other hand, very many that we can eliminate as simply too improbable to be worth a second thought.[13] In any case, we are talking about what one author has called "the necessity for choice," which should be interpreted to mean *reasonable* choice.

Though it is good to be imaginative and important to keep an open mind, it is imperative to avoid basing far-reaching policy decisions on contin-

[12] The distinguished French political economist, Bertrand de Jouvenel, has recently attempted to give something of the status of a movement to the study of what he calls *futuribles*. A conference on the subject was held at the Yale Law School, 4-6 December 1964.

[13] The Russians' putting the missiles into Cuba is so often mentioned as ostensible proof to the contrary that it is worth pointing out that our government had several times prior to the event warned the Soviet government not to do what it subsequently did do. Did not these warnings reflect a sense at least of "finite possibility"? There were many prominent Americans in and out of the government who thought it much more than a finite possibility, and the Pentagon had in fact prepared appropriate "contingency plans." Krushchev had simply chosen to be guided not by our verbal admonitions but by a number of other indices, including his measurement of President Kennedy at the June 1961 meeting in Vienna—where he had badgered the latter about the Bay of Pigs episode—and by the administration's permissiveness concerning the prolonged Soviet buildup of "defensive" installations in Cuba. See Elie Abel, *The Missile Crisis*, Lippincott, New York, 1966, pp. 11-42.

gencies which can be called conceivable only because someone has conceived of them. In this era when the memory of Winston Churchill is still fresh, it is worth recalling that he made his reputation as a prophet mostly by insisting doggedly in the several years before World War II that Hitlerism was incompatible with peace. It required at the time no great imagination to come to that conclusion—only the sagacity to concentrate on the important facts and, in that instance, the courage to face and publicly to insist upon the altogether unpleasant implications of those facts.

Change is something to which we are not unaccustomed. We have even learned, through experience, many practical ways for dealing with it. For one thing, we squeeze into our military budget —near the 50 billion dollar mark even before the late-1965 increase in our commitment to Vietnam— provision for many unpleasant contingencies, more than a few of which we might be justified in rating individually as most unlikely. Also, change does not always happen suddenly. There is often ample opportunity to reappraise the developing situation in the light of new circumstances. In doing so it is always a good preparatory exercise to have assessed carefully the recent past. For the relatively near term to which we are confining ourselves in this analysis, many (though certainly not all) of the most important factors that have strongly characterized the last twenty years are likely still to be valid.

IV · The Attenuation of Incentives For "Going First"

WE REFERRED in our opening remarks to another feature of the strategic environment of today—and one that will probably be of increasing moment in the near future—which must have a great and possibly decisive influence in reducing the danger of uncontrolled escalation following from any local outbreak. It is the rapidly diminishing (that is, in 1966) advantage and thus incentive of going first in any *strategic* exchange. Until the early or middle sixties the advantage of striking first in such an exchange promised to be so huge and so obviously decisive that it was itself probably the chief factor that would have made for rapid escalation to general war following outbreak of hostilties between the Soviet Union and the United States. With the recent extraordinary diminution in vulnerability of the retaliatory forces, however, most conspicuously on the American side, but presumably progressing also on the other side, the incentive for going first has drastically declined.

Among the situations reflecting this reduction of incentive is the well-known targeting dilemma with which American strategic analysts have lately been preoccupied. The general consensus approving the no-cities targeting philosophy—on the ground that in a swift-moving war there is no strategic utility in destroying cities ("hostages are better than

corpses") and plenty of positive incentive for
mutually avoiding them—is overlaid with a growing concern that counterforce or "damage-limiting"
targets (that is, the enemy's strategic retaliatory
forces, destruction of which limits potential damage to oneself) may prove of steadily diminishing
attractiveness. The reason is that even at best the
residual damage-producing capabilities of the enemy after an American counterforce strike are
likely to remain huge.[1] From being a good damage-
limiting system, a strategy stressing counterforce
targets may have a hard time maintaining its claim
to being the least bad system. The strong moral
and political inhibitions Americans have consistently felt in the nuclear era against hitting first
with nuclear weapons will now be supported on the
strategic level by cold calculations that will impress
one with the lack of urgency about doing so. The
same incentives for not doing so will be even more
obvious on the Soviet side.

We have also noted that with respect to *tactical*
use of nuclear weapons the advantages of first use
will in some situations still appear great, and no

---

[1] In his statement of January 25, 1966 before a House Armed
Services subcommittee, Secretary McNamara included the following remarks: ". . . against the forces we expect the Soviets to
have during the next decade, it will be virtually impossible for
us to be able to ensure anything approaching complete protection
for our population, no matter now large the general nuclear war
forces we were to provide, including even the hypothetical possibility of striking first. . . . The Soviets have the technical and
economic capacity to prevent us from achieving a posture which
could keep our fatalities below some tens of millions. . . ." *New
York Times*, January 26, 1966.

radical diminution of these advantages is in sight. Tactical air forces especially tend to be so vulnerable to surprise nuclear attack as to create in themselves a strong incentive for "going nuclear" in any substantial hostilities where both sides might possess nuclear weapons. Obviously, these observations do not apply to small "demonstration" use of nuclear weapons.

The implications of the crucial change just described in the general strategic environment of our times appear to be quite generally overlooked. From time to time events occur which alter profoundly all previous appreciations of strategic essentials, and this seems to be one of them. It is not an inevitable change, for improvements in missile performance that might tend to nullify the advantages of some kind of hardening are certainly conceivable. But we have plenty of experience from the past to remind us that technology always moves along a broad front, and also there is more than a trick or two available for the defenses. It seems in the net fairly safe to predict that the degree of advantage that was until recently thought to accrue to the side making a surprise strategic attack—where it could hope to wipe out the retaliatory force of the opponent with near impunity—is gone, and is not likely to return among opponents no more disparate in power than the United States and the Soviet Union have recently become. At any rate, it is not easy to imagine a future government *being confident* that it can make so effectively one-sided an attack, especially since this kind of confidence was not conspicuous in the past even under circumstances when it was much more warranted than it is ever likely to be again. As Secretary McNamara stated the dilemma from the American point of view, early in 1963:

> I *do not* believe we are either unimaginative, or lacking in skill, but I do believe that a careful assessment of the probable increases in the Soviet nuclear power as estimated by the experienced intelligence evaluators in our Government indicate that power will increase in such ways, particularly in such types, that there will not be a possibility for us to build a force that can destroy that power to such a degree that there will not remain elements so large as to cause severe damage to our Nation in retaliation for our destructive effort directed against that power.[2]

The inelegance of the syntax may be excused in view of the comprehensiveness and pointedness of the statement, which illustrates what is meant by saying that the opportunities for a "first strike" are rapidly diminishing if not already gone. It explains, in other words, the otherwise bizarre idea that in today's world it is more feasible to provide "second strike" than "first strike" capabilities.

---

[2] *Department of Defense Appropriations for 1964*, Part I, subcommittee of the Committee on Appropriations, House of Representatives, Washington, D. C., 1963, p. 341.

That is, he who strikes first had better get a very much larger proportion of the enemy's retaliatory forces than, under modern conditions, he has much right to expect. From that point of view the prospects for a first strike must certainly look a good deal less feasible to the Russians than they do to us.

V · What Is the Enemy Up To?

It is amazing but true that practically all public discussion concerning the appropriate time for introducing nuclear weapons in tactical operations has neglected to consider the enemy's intention. The criteria mentioned have usually been mechanical phenomena, like the scale of hostilities reached or the rate at which territory is being yielded. One would rather expect the first consideration to be: What is the enemy up to?

This anomalous situation cannot be ascribed to the probable obscurity of the opponent's intention, since upon the outbreak of any real hostilities his intention is likely to be fairly obvious. It would very likely be reflected in the manifest scale and character of his military preparations, and even more in the scale of his attack. Certainly a deliberate major aggression will look very different from the kind of probing actions out of which "accidental" wars are supposed to grow.

For the sake of deterrence, and also to reassure our allies, it would seem appropriate to relate flexibility of response mainly *to discrimination of enemy intent.* That would make more sense than saying, as we have in effect said in the past: "We will use conventional weapons until we find ourselves losing." If it is true that the possibility of a deliberate massive Soviet attack against Western Europe is exceedingly remote, so much the more reason for

avoiding ambiguity concerning our response to it.
Most of the public debate about how the United
States should resist Soviet aggression has in fact
concerned itself with this particularly remote possibility, where withholding of nuclear weapons
would have the least justification.

A deliberate and massive enemy attack would
also minimize the inhibitions of our political leaders about using nuclear weapons. The specter of
their being paralyzed by such inhibitions seems to
worry some people, though curiously they are often
the same people who do not want to use nuclear
weapons anyway. The pertinent argument has been:
"We should be ready to fight the first stages of a
war in Europe conventionally if only because commitment to hostilities on a large scale is the only
way we can be sure of being able to bring ourselves
to use nuclear weapons when needed." This attitude surely reflects, among other things, lack of
sensitivity to the shock effects of a major military
attack which disrupts a condition of peace. One
might add that to follow such a policy would be the
best way to ensure that if nuclear weapons were
indeed used they would be used on a large and
extremely destructive scale rather than on a controlled demonstration scale.

But are we really justified in assigning an exceedingly low order of probability to a deliberate and
massive enemy attack? In discussing military contingencies in Europe, such an attack is what military specialists have talked about most of the time.

Americans who gratefully accept the idea that sudden general or strategic war between the great nuclear powers has become extremely improbable nevertheless seem to find unsettling the effects of that conclusion upon their estimate of the probabilities of war on any lesser scale. Many indeed seem to be tacitly (and occasionally even explicitly) assuming that the probability of *some* kind of war occurring has remained basically fixed—after all, there have always been wars—and thus if general war is now less likely, it must follow that limited war (including quite large-scale limited war) has become more so! Others, not quite so mechanistic in their conceptions, nevertheless argue that because the defender cannot meaningfully threaten "massive retaliation" in the event of local transgressions by the aggressor, the latter's inducement to undertake such transgressions is greatly increased. Naturally, most of these arguments have not reached the ear of the wider public, but among the now substantial band of specialists they are common.

One might suppose that the same factors that dissuade the Russians from making a strategic attack upon the United States work also to dissuade them from attempting a deliberate, large-scale land attack upon or invasion of Western Europe. That, after all, would be the kind of operation that would come closest to triggering the general war that they are, with good reason, desperately anxious to avoid. Besides, it is difficult to discover what meaningful incentives the Russians might have for attempting to conquer Western Europe—especially incentives that are even remotely commensurate with the risks. The idea that through such conquest they might be tempted to gain important economic advantages, such as absorption of the productive plant of Western Europe, was never worth serious consideration even when the Russians were much further behind industrially than they are now.

It has been a recurrent notion among American military planners (and some French) that if the Russians got into a major war with the NATO powers, they would try to spare Western Europe from atomic destruction in order to be able to capture and utilize its productive plant at war's end. This idea seems never to have occurred to the Russians, who instead developed under Khrushchev the "hostage" principle of defense, that is, the principle that MRBMs directed against Western Europe were as good, or almost as good, a measure against the United States as ICBMs directed against our homeland. The Russian view is certainly more reasonable than the above-mentioned contrasting one. Modern nuclear wars are not likely to be fought for plunder, which in any case would prove difficult to absorb and especially to transfer. The Russians, incidentally, have had much direct experience in this matter, especially in the futility of attempting to transfer productive facilities from Germany to their own country following World War II. They have reason to know

that the kind of aggrandizement that truly in-
creases national power is not likely, in modern
times, to be the result of foreign conquest.

Thus we are forced again to the conclusion that
large-scale tactical war in Europe, if it occurs at
all, must come about through escalation from Soviet probing actions. According to Soviet ideology
it could occur also, and in fact almost exclusively,
as a result of an attack by us upon them. We
naturally rate the chances of the latter event very
low. Insofar, however, as the Russians could conceivably act by anticipating (or "pre-empting" in
technical jargon) what they considered to be a
menacing act by us, we have to examine the possibilities of their totally misjudging our intentions
in crisis situations.

It would seem that the most fruitful question
we could ask about the use of nuclear weapons in
tactical operations, expecially in Europe, would be:
How could their use, or non-use, or threat of use
affect the prospects for the occurrence of escalation
from small-scale to large-scale combat? We ought
not to be talking, certainly not initially, about
using a great many nuclear weapons; that is a possibility that occurs only after a conflict has already
graduated to large proportions and corresponding
intensity. We should be interested mainly in seeing
how it can be prevented from ever reaching such
proportions. We are interested, in other words, in
the prevention, through deterrence, of escalation—
though not for one moment are we less interested in

the comparable prevention of initial hostilities.

In that connection, we have to observe that the phrase "if deterrence fails" rolls rather too trippingly off the tongues of some of those many defense specialists whose work requires them to think about what happens in actual combat. Certainly the phrase begs many questions. For the purpose of deciding what our defense posture should be, one has to consider some all-important intermediate questions, like: *Why* should deterrence fail? *How* could it fail? How can we keep it from failing? To the last of these questions one should always be able to give a positive answer. Unless we are dealing with utter madmen, there is no conceivable reason why in any necessary showdown with the Soviet Union, appropriate manipulations of force and threats of force, certainly coordinated with more positive diplomatic maneuvers, cannot bring about deterrence. That is one respect in which the world is utterly different now from what it was in 1939 or 1914, when deterrence, however effective temporarily, had the final intrinsic weakness that one side or both did not truly fear what we would now call general war.

VI · *The Status Quo as a Standard*

THE SUGGESTION made in the last chapter that to-day we should be able reliably to avoid major war without politically disastrous retreats implies the existence of two circumstances: (1) that we have a (preferably) commanding superiority in our overall force posture or at least a position that we cannot be induced to recognize as significantly inferior; and (2) that there be some standard in the world by which both sides can, within reasonable limits, simultaneously distinguish acceptable behavior from the intolerably deviant kind.

On territorial issues, which historically have been the great provokers of war, the standard that comes at once to mind is naturally the status quo. Thus the two circumstances described above are rather closely related, because the degree of superiority that enables one to stand against aggressive encroachments upon one's territory or that of allies to whom one is closely committed will normally be less than that necessary for the other side to have in order to gain changes by aggression. Obviously other characteristics matter too, above all determination in aggressiveness or in withstanding aggression, but the distinction between superiority and inferiority is, when sharp enough, hard to obliterate. Historically the aggressors have been those who have been ready to make the most of a superiority that might indeed be only temporary or localized, but they have usually sought to satisfy themselves that that superiority was real rather than merely fictitious.[1]

"What *is* superiority?" is a question that has always had more complications than appeared on the surface. Napoleon's famous dictum that "the moral is to the material as three is to one" was a shrewd but even in his time a fairly standard reflection on the perennial unwisdom of merely counting up guns or divisions or whatnot. When Nelson met Villeneuve at Trafalgar, both men were agreed on which side was superior, though the French admiral clearly had more ships and guns under his command.

In our own time the problem has become enormously more complicated as a result of the special intolerability of nuclear devastation, and our quotation from Secretary McNamara (Chap. 4) expresses just one additional facet of the problem. However, it is perhaps fortunate for the United States that the difficulty in being content with the traditional indices of superiority seems to grow more or less in proportion to the degree of sophistication with which one approaches the problem, and crisis situations appear to induce on both sides regression to relatively primitive evaluations. Prior

---

[1] A qualified exception is the Japanese decision in 1941 to make war against the United States, about whose basic superiority they had no illusions, but the possibility of a local temporary superiority was clearly envisioned and, in fact, actually attained. The subject is well treated in Robert J. C. Butow, *Tojo and the Coming of the War*, Princeton University Press, Princeton, 1961, especially ch. 11.

to the Cuban crisis there was a special danger that, given our official national preoccupation with the importance of conventional forces, we would talk ourselves into a conviction of inferiority regarding the local situation in Berlin. But fortunately the Russians put us right by their behavior during and after that crisis. Superiority, they in effect argued, was not as divisible either regionally or in terms of weaponry as we had supposed; also, the degree of superiority that they were willing to credit us with was enough and to spare for our purpose, which both in the Caribbean and in Berlin was essentially the maintenance of the status quo.

This brings us again to the special importance of the status quo, which in the past has too often been rejected, especially by intellectuals, because it always fell short of the ideal. But whatever limitations the status quo may have, there has always been a certain sanctity about things-as-they-happen-to-be precisely because things-as-they-happen-to-be are in certain matters, especially boundaries, conspicuously inseparable from peace, or at least from nonfighting. The essence of President Kennedy's case against the Soviet missiles in Cuba was, as stated in his famous speech of October 22, 1962, that they represented a sudden change in the status quo of military power: ". . . this secret, swift, and extraordinary buildup of Communist missiles . . . this sudden clandestine decision . . . is a deliberately provocative and unjustified change in the status quo. . . ."

It happens that the maintenance of the status quo is usually also supported by international law, which is to say by written international agreements, rights of prescription, custom, etc. Everyone knows that there are often disagreements, sometimes serious, about what international law really stipulates (for example, is the MacMahon line the legally correct boundary between India and China?), but superimposed on these disagreements is the very strong feeling that, if there is fighting, whatever situation prevailed before fighting began was somehow in some degree right *because* it was compatible with nonfighting, and whoever started the fighting was, for the reason of doing so, blameworthy. Actually this strong feeling is itself dignified by being enshrined in international law, which in the United Nations Charter and various other general or multilateral treaties specifically forbids resort to force except in self-defense.

We are accustomed to some states being called status quo powers, and to other states being called revisionist. These distinctions usually mean that the states so indicated not only have incompatible desires concerning the future of the world, but markedly different attitudes concerning the acceptability of the present. Nevertheless, however much revisionist powers may dislike existing boundaries or other arrangements, they must not find them intolerable; they share with the status quo powers a common perception of the awful significance of stepping over those lines which at any one time represent the general working consensus concerning boundaries. To step over them is to invoke military conflict, with its inevitable costs and risks. The abortive attempt in 1965 of the Pakistanis to take Kashmir had to be a resort to force, and its quick failure brought an almost predetermined settlement which had nothing to do with the validity of their claims—return to the status quo ante.

In Germany today, both sides are at the same time revisionist in some respects and status quo in others. Both recognize the status quo to be, by formal stipulation, temporary; but since they cannot agree on how to go about changing it, the status quo has acquired a powerful sanction of legitimacy. The Russians want to make permanent the existing division between East and West Germany, but they would also like to change the status of West Berlin. The Western powers, on the other hand, are committed to holding their position in Berlin, but they are revisionist in being committed, at least in theory, to seeing Germany reunified. Actually, almost no people besides the Germans really desire to see Germany reunified, and even among the Germans the subject is of widely varying interest, with real intensity of feeling being mostly limited to the Berliners and the East Germans.[2]

The United States and its allies have customarily shown more relaxation about the existing state of affairs than the Russians, but that is less a matter of the tolerability or intolerability of the existing conditions to each side than it is of the basic philos-

[2] See the very perceptive article on this subject by Karl Loewenstein, "Berlin Revisited: Thoughts on Unification," *Current History*, May 1966, pp. 263ff.

ophy of each concerning its appropriate posture towards the possibility of securing change. The Russians, being doctrinaire activists, are committed to relentlessness in securing all possible changes favorable to them so long as no undue risks are involved; it is the *possibility* of favorable change which alone will determine for them how "insupportable" the present really is. The United States and its allies, on the other hand, have no such compulsion to exploit whatever marginal opportunities for change may come their way, and in general prefer not to stir up trouble. This is the key difference between the side that pushes and the side that does not become really aroused until it is pushed. Thus the latter determines by its response what the former will find tolerable or intolerable. It must therefore be staunch about resisting, and must resist small and apparently "trivial" encroachments as well as big ones, for the former have often proved (on the part of the Russians) to be deliberate probes.

Inasmuch as, in the present instance, both sides in Europe definitely prefer a not too unhappy peace to any kind of war, they appear reconciled to continuing indefinitely what was once recognized by both to be a temporary state of affairs. This indispensable consensus does not exclude what we used to call "peaceful change," which is to say the pursuit and accomplishment of more stable (that is, mutually satisfactory) arrangements through various forms of accommodation reached by negotiation. And naturally the status quo we are committed to defend concerns mainly international territorial arrangements, not domestic conditions. The latter we know to be desperate over a very large part of the world, and we have already devoted much of our wealth and power to helping to alleviate them.

There seems little doubt that, in Europe at least, the territorial status quo has gained markedly in sanctity in the nuclear era. The responsibility for upsetting an existing state of peace becomes much heavier when that disturbance has a measurable chance of setting off nuclear weapons. More to the point, the side contemplating aggression must make its estimate of the outcome in the knowledge that if major war results, the possibility of its achieving gains that outweigh penalties is by orders of magnitude more dubious than it has ever before appeared to any aggressor. Thus, the stability of the present situation rests largely on the unprecedented *lack of ambiguity* between what is at worst an unhappy situation—and to most of the major parties not even that—and what on the other hand would be obviously quite awful.

This condition is reflected, for example, in the practically universal persuasion in Germany today that reunification must be accomplished *ohne Krieg* —without war. Dissatisfaction with the existing state of affairs there no doubt is, but the kind of irredentism that played so large a part in producing the two world wars does not exist today in Europe. Whatever their ignorance about the specific effects of nuclear weapons, the Europeans have learned quite enough about war generally; they also know enough about how much worse it would be with large-scale use of nuclear weapons to be clear that they cannot afford flammable irredentas. However, they have also been playing the game long enough to know that the present favorable situation, which convincingly promises peace despite the most potent ideological cleavage in Europe since at least the age of the religious wars, depends on maintaining the marvelous clarity of choice between nonwar and destruction. This in brief explains why many sensible and knowledgeable Europeans could be so alarmed at the deliberate American effort to make the nuclear threat *more ambiguous*—which is probably an inevitable result and certainly a valid interpretation of the effort to expand "options"—rather than less so.

One should notice also the kind of asymmetry between aggressor and defender that normally eases the problem of decision for the latter. One should not push this point too far. The aggressor leaders may well have the disposition to bear with ease the special burdens of aggressive action, but those burdens are nevertheless real and formidable. Even Hitler—in disposition the archetype of the aggressor—was prepared in 1936 to withdraw the forces he had sent to reoccupy the right bank of the Rhine, if the French had only shown an inclination to move.[3] It was not alone relevant that the French at

[3] One must note the recent and remarkable interpretation, novel but hardly scholarly, of why the French did not move

that time were militarily superior; Hitler knew that it was he who stood out as the one who was disturbing the status quo in a way that could produce a war. It is obvious that for most governments, conspicuously including our own, the problem of deciding to use force is enormously eased if they find themselves in the position of resisting aggression rather than perpetrating it. Something of this quality is reflected in the vast difference between the behavior of the same U.S. government in the Bay of Pigs episode of April 1961 and in the Cuban crisis of October 1962.

A kind of misplaced recognition of this factor is reflected in the repeated reference to the problem, in a crisis, of "shooting first." Thus, it is sometimes alleged that in trying to keep us out of Berlin the Russians could play a very clever game by putting us in a position where we have to fire the first shot to force our way through an obstacle blocking access. This point has certainly been exaggerated. The question of who has actually pulled the trigger first on a hand weapon like a rifle is likely to prove an obscure detail that cannot be objectively recalled to anyone's complete satisfaction. The erection of the obstacle in the first place, in violation of prevailing rules of access, would be a much more conspicuous departure from the status quo and thus

---

offered by Henry Owen of the U.S. State Department in his "NATO Strategy: What is Past is Prologue," *Foreign Affairs*, XLIII (July 1965) 682-690. Mr. Owen has been a strong and influential proponent of building up conventional forces in Europe.

the initiating act of aggression. One form of transgression easily outweighs the other. When Hitler charged that it was the Poles who had begun World War II by opening fire on German soldiers, nobody outside Germany believed him. Yet even if the statement had been literally true and had been believed, the fact that the dangerous situation in which the firing occurred had been created entirely by Hitler would have determined the relevant attitudes of other peoples and statesmen.

It should not now be necessary to add that a deliberate massive attack by one great power against the forces of another has always in modern times been an extraordinarily serious and deeply shocking event, and that it is bound to be even more so in a world that knows nuclear weapons. However, the debate on nuclear versus conventional strategies or "options" has so sharply focused men's minds on the dread consequences of using nuclear weapons tactically that the very act of aggression that might invoke these possibilities has been excessively deflated by comparison. In many recent discussions of the issue, the fact of aggression seems to be given about the emotional loading of an enemy prank. It is supposed to be contained in a manner that is effective but at the same time tolerant and wise. The argument above that we should be unambiguous at least about opposing with nuclear arms any *deliberate and massive* Soviet attack in Europe is, in one sense, only a plea to resume treating such aggression with the seriousness it deserves.

VII · On Enemy Capabilities Versus Intentions

THE DEFENSE community has long been ambivalent concerning the question of whether our defense preparations and planning must be responsive to enemy capabilities or to enemy intentions. The answer has to be—and inevitably is—"to both."

Enemy capabilities, to the (probably considerable) degree that we succeed in measuring them, certainly provide us the basic raw data about our defense needs. In the kinds of forces we consider to matter most, we are able, and at least until recently have been determined, to be comfortably superior, and we measure our success in achieving that superiority by making the obvious comparisons between their strength and ours. On the other hand, it is also clear that our defense efforts, large as they are, are considerably below what they could be if we became really alarmed about our chances of keeping the peace. Surely, then, our composure argues a persuasion that the opponent does not mean to have a war with us, at least not soon. Actually, when it comes to deciding not only the magnitude but also the character of our preparations, we correctly and necessarily let ourselves be guided by our beliefs, guesses, or convictions about what the opponent is now or may in the future be up to.[1]

[1] An example of special current interest involves the questions of when and to what extent to begin deployment of an anti-

It has, on the other hand, never been quite respectable among military people to admit that important planning judgments are based on our conceptions of enemy intentions. Those intentions are often held to be easily changeable, and our conceptions of them are generally considered to be more subjective, tenuous, and faulty than our conceptions about the size and quality of his military forces. We can also be in error about the latter, but normally we expend much more effort in seeking knowledge of enemy forces, and the data we examine in that pursuit are certainly more tangible and therefore more apparently "objective" than they are in the other case. It is often alleged, besides, that the opponent's military capabilities are the best clue we have to his intentions, but the core of truth in that assertion depends on the discrimination and sensitivity with which we scrutinize his military expenditures and capabilities. It is not only how much he spends on military force that matters, but also how he chooses to spend it, and why. What is the significance, for example, of the long observed fact that a very large proportion of the sums the Russians have spent on "air power" has habitually gone into air defense at the cost of air offense?

Intelligence about enemy capabilities can be and is generally presented in hard figures, and in de-

---

ballistic-missile defense suitable for use against Soviet capabilities. The difficulties in making these decision are enhanced by, among other considerations, the inevitably limited effectiveness and the extremely high cost of such defenses.

scriptions of physical things in terms that almost everyone interested in the matter feels he can understand. The knowledge may be difficult in accessibility, but only in its refinements is it especially esoteric. By contrast, the knowledge that enables our appropriate experts to make shrewd surmises of Soviet intentions is highly esoteric, although most of the relevant source materials are readily available in completely open sources. These carefully trained experts, who have learned how to weight and organize the data revealing Soviet beliefs, fixations, aspirations, and problems, will also have difficulties in communicating their knowledge or insights to policy-makers. The latter are as often as not distrustful of the reliability of this particular brand of scholarship. Nevertheless, the message does tend to get through, though inevitably with some delay and distortion.

In any case, we must accept the following two points: First, official American estimates of U.S. military requirements are inevitably deeply colored by the policy-makers' conceptions of the opponent's *intentions*—which suggests that we ought to keep these conceptions as explicit as possible and subject to continuous, systematic review. Second, our capabilities, and the opponent's are important less for determining who would win a major nuclear conflict—which neither he nor we will care to see proceed to any conclusive test—than for their bearing (which under different circumstances may be great or small) on the questions that immediately arise concerning any projected crisis: What will the opponent be likely to *do* under certain contingencies? How will he respond to what we do? What, under these considerations, can we bring ourselves to do?

In our spontaneous, entirely intuited, ambivalent, and highly uncertain answers to questions akin to these are wrapped up all our fears and doubts about escalation. *The control of escalation is an exercise in deterrence.* We try first and foremost to deter the opponent from doing that which will oblige us to threaten or resort to any use of arms; if he nevertheless persists and a conflict starts, we try to deter him from enlarging it, or even from continuing it. Deterrence, at any level, thus naturally means inducing the enemy to confine his military actions to levels far below those delimited by his capabilities.

VIII · *The New and Different Europe*

It SHOULD be easy to win agreement that Europe is a vastly different place as concerns the probability of major war from what it was in 1914, or in 1939. It is also worth remembering that Europe in 1939 was altogether different from Europe in 1914. With the public emotions and attitudes prevailing in 1914, it was all too easy for the mediocre men controlling certain governments to start a great war. It took, on the other hand, the evil genius of a Hitler to start another world war in 1939. Among the major participating powers the first war began with great floods of nationalist enthusiasm, which endured, despite enormous casualties, for two whole years—enabling Britain during that time, for example, to send to France well over a million men who were recruited on a strictly volunteer basis. World War II, on the other hand, began with a deeply contrasting spirit of glumness and dismay, not less in Berlin than in Paris or London.[1]

Today all Europeans, including especially the Russians, have had the experience of two world wars to condition their attitudes toward the kinds of political problems that previously produced wars, and also toward war itself. Those wars are seen by the peoples of Europe simply as immense catastrophes, devoid of traces of glory such as clung to

[1] An extraordinarily good, brief essay contrasting the two world wars in these respects is a review article by the distinguished

former wars. The idea that there could be any object apart from sheer survival worth the fighting of another great war is plainly not there. One of the many indices of the remarkably complete rejection of the war-fighting past, with all its bloodshed among nations of essentially a common civilization, is the extraordinary degree to which the French-German reconciliation has reached deeply into the attitudes of the respective peoples. It is far from being merely a creation of a few people at the top. And the people at the top, one should recall, no longer derive from that hereditary aristocracy, with its peculiarly militaristic and chauvinistic way of life surviving from ages past, that ruled the great empires of central and eastern Europe until World War I. That class has simply disappeared.

Added to the experience of two world wars, with the vast changes they produced, is now the nuclear bomb, a device which pretty nearly universally removes any lingering doubts about the catastrophic nature of major war. It seems therefore to change completely the requirements of security, in a way which for most Europeans tends to spell relaxation rather than the reverse. Preoccupied as they are with their unprecedented prosperity, and aware also of their diminished status as compared with the two superpowers, they are content to enjoy what seem to them to be the benefits of this change,

British historian, Michael Howard. Incidentally reviewing a book by A. J. P. Taylor, it is entitled "Lest We Forget," *Encounter*, January 1964, pp. 61-67.

as for example the possibility of avoidance or very lukewarm tolerance of conscription.

There is obviously a negative note in all this. Some have pointed out that the Europe we are describing is too pacifically inclined not only to start a war but also to resist resolutely any major aggression from the East. The Europeans may, these observers say, loudly clamor for putting a tough nuclear face on our common provisions for defense, but in a crisis any threat to use nuclear weapons is far more likely to frighten than to reassure them. This point has frequently been made in support of building up and giving greater emphasis to conventional forces in Europe.

One trouble with this argument is not that its basic premise is necessarily untrue, but that it does not conform rigorously enough to that premise. When and if a situation arises in which the Europeans reject out of fear any thought of using or threatening to use nuclear weapons in their own defense, they are not likely to be prepared to fight a major war conventionally either, especially inasmuch as no commitment to conventional defense can go much beyond the suggestion to *begin* fighting conventionally. However, even if we could promise what is in fact impossible to promise— that we could and would *keep* large-scale hostilities conventional—a third world war in any case means to most Europeans the death of Europe. If a conventional buildup is advocated, as it has been advocated, on the grounds that it will buy more backbone for our allies in a crisis, we really ought to look very carefully at the promised payoff to see whether the alleged extra margin of backbone justifies the very considerable extra cost.

If these observations seem to strike at the basic philosophy of NATO, it may simply be because we fail to recall the Europeans' original image of NATO. What NATO originally meant was above all an American commitment to Europe—an essentially unilateral guarantee in the guise of an alliance of equals—sufficient to *deter* the Soviets from aggression. Everything else was mainly supplementary and, it was hoped, not too expensive "burden sharing." Changes in these attitudes as a result of European recovery have been among the Europeans, rather marginal and superficial. The American drive—especially under the Kennedy and Johnson administrations—for greater efficiency in the NATO defense structure, for greater rationality in war-fighting plans, and for various related values has always seemed to most informed Europeans somewhat beside the point, and, in so far as it involved a certain measure of hectoring, has been decidedly negative in its results. The essence of NATO to the European has been, to repeat, the American presence in and commitment to Europe, alongside of which nothing else greatly mattered. De Gaulle seems to have other ideas, but the difference mostly concerns what he now considers the excessive cost in his values of the American presence—as opposed to simple commitment.

The other side of the coin is that the Soviet Union has for a long time seemed to most Europeans to be offering no serious threat of aggression. There is still, to be sure, a deep ideological cleavage between the Soviet Union and the NATO Powers, and there is the continuing territorial division of Germany. Yet even in these respects the situation today looks somehow less grim than it did only a few years ago.

There has been for one thing the Sino-Soviet split, which has not only survived but in fact deepened despite a change of leadership in the Soviet Union. Some Americans have cautioned that the net effect of such a split could be to our disadvantage. This idea has unquestionably some shade of justification, yet one wonders how much it simply reflects the modern "cult of the ominous." Each side needs, no doubt, to be in competition with the other to prove that it is orthodox in its support of "national liberation" movements; but how does the split affect the *risks* that each is willing to take in offering that proof? In the net the division seems to have played an important part in modifying favorably from our point of view the behavior of the Soviet Union, and possibly also that of Communist China. It has also highlighted usefully for us the contrast between an unreconstructed and rigidly doctrinaire China and a more flexible, obviously changing Russia.[2]

[2] On the subject of "The Soviet Union and the Sino-Soviet Dispute," see the "Statement" by Thomas W. Wolfe of The RAND

The Cuban crisis of 1962, which a British statesman has called the "Cuban Trafalgar," also had a
major effect on subsequent Soviet conduct, obviously because it shocked the Soviet leaders into
awareness that the United States was prepared for
military confrontations even over issues that, while
gravely important, were not necessarily desperate
for the United States. Equally important, it gave
American political leaders new insights into some
relevant aspects of Soviet conduct—insights they
did not have to accept on faith from experts—one
result of which will be to reduce for some time any
leverage the Russians might otherwise have sought
to derive from bellicosity. Less than a year after
the crisis the Russians proved willing to sign the
same test-ban treaty that they had previously rejected with derision.

There is also the clear fact that the European
satellites of the Soviet Union have achieved much
greater autonomy in both their domestic and foreign affairs than we used to think was possible for
them. If local Communist leaders prove difficult or
unmalleable, world revolution as a goal must glit-
ter somewhat less in Moscow eyes.

About the Soviet Union itself we have already
had occasion to observe (a) that while it has been

Corporation, before the Subcommittee on the Far East and the
Pacific, Committee on Foreign Affairs, House of Representatives,
Washington, D. C., March 11, 1965. For the significance to Ameri-
can policy of developments in the Soviet Union, see especially
Marshall D. Shulman, *Beyond the Cold War*, Yale University
Press, New Haven, 1966.

and continues to be aggressive politically, with a
good deal of bluster and even occasional threats,
its military behavior has always been extremely
cautious; (b) that it has not shown any interest in
conquering Western Europe, especially since it has
gained enough confidence in its own strength to
worry less about being invaded from the West; and
(c) that though it would clearly like to see West
Berlin fall into the Communist camp, it is equally
clearly unwilling to undertake any real risk of hostilities with the United States to bring about that
event.

Obviously, these few pages on what has happened to Europe since 1914 (we have hardly more
than mentioned China) can only suggest the main
trends and indicate the relevance of those trends to
our main problem. One essential point to note is
that the imperfections of any instrument designed
to deter an opponent from aggression must be considered against the real burden of weight that that
instrument must bear, that is, against the real degree of threat which it is supposed effectively to oppose. Inasmuch as the importance of NATO has
been primarily in establishing the American presence in Europe, the imperfections of the operations and mechanisms of NATO must be measured
against that fact—and also against the fact that the
Soviet Union has shown itself on the record to be
less than avid to pursue a career of nuclear black-
mail against either the Western Europeans or ourselves.

Again we need to anticipate the reminder that the world changes. So indeed it does, and we have already discussed that earlier.[3] We have been describing in this brief section some trends that are (a) relevant to our inquiry about escalation, (b) of long-term duration, and (c) basic rather than merely superficial.

[Incidentally, with respect to the Cuban missile crisis mentioned again above (p. 94), when this book first went to press I thought it quite unnecessary to point out that against an opponent given to probing an occasional *confrontation* was an essential ingredient in deterrence. However, a review-article by I. F. Stone in the *New York Review of Books* some three and a half years after the event (concerning the book by Elie Abel cited on p. 61) was one long expression of horror that President Kennedy had had the audacity to make this confrontation. Mr. Stone did not hesitate to attribute the late President's action to his vanity. In view of the extremely favorable outcome of that confrontation, one would have thought it incumbent upon Mr. Stone at least to speculate on what might have been the consequences had Kennedy lacked the courage to make it.]

[3] See above, pp. 60-62.

IX · How Big an Attack?

WE HAVE suggested if not concluded that the contingency that ought to be put at or near the lowest level of probability is a deliberate, massive attack of the Soviet field forces against the NATO line in central Europe. This happens to be the kind of war outbreak in Europe that has been the most discussed in official circles and that no doubt has absorbed far the major part of NATO planning. This is not necessarily paradoxical if it is the existence of NATO that makes, or helps to make, the probability of Soviet attack so low. Massive attack is indeed the way major wars in Europe have traditionally begun in modern times—prior to the era of nuclear weapons. Today, however, it is virtually impossible to discover in the real world the considerations that could make the Soviet leaders undertake such an attack in the face of the minimum gains and the enormous risks they would be incurring—risks that are certainly not slighted in their published military and political doctrine.

What sorts of changes should one take into account that might basically alter this assessment?

Perhaps one should allow for the possibility that the risks presently deterring the Russians from massive westward aggression may in the future appear to them to have been virtually eliminated—as for example by the complete disintegration of NATO. This could presumably involve the departure of the U.S. presence from Europe (which, for the purpose of our present strategic analysis, would effectively put the matter beyond our terms of reference). However, if one wants to speculate, one should also remember that it would make a considerable difference *what* had caused the disintegration of NATO. It might have collapsed mostly because fear of Russia had been too far reduced, in which case a revival of danger might perhaps permit NATO—possibly in a good deal more efficient form—to be reconstituted. One would also still have to find those hard-to-discover incentives for Russian *military* expansion westward.

One should also consider the possibility that relevant Soviet military doctrine will change materially. It has clearly been undergoing some modification in recent years. In general, Soviet doctrine has been much more conservative than ours, as reflected, in one relevant example, in its skepticism and even derision regarding American propensities for making frequent and easy distinctions between limited and general, and especially between non-nuclear and nuclear, war. There has been some slight Soviet yielding of ground in these points of doctrine over the last two years, but the confidence of various American observers that the Russians are simply "six or seven years behind us"—with the clear implication that after the appropriate lapse of time they will be about where we are now —seems to be quite unwarranted.[1]

[1] See especially the following: Leon Gouré, *Notes on the Second*

For one thing, where really are we now? People who make the judgment just cited usually represent a distinct school of thought—a school which places maximum emphasis on conventional capabilities, and which considers the logic of its position so compelling as to be self-evident. Yet the fact that substantial parts even of the U.S. defense community have not been won over suggests that the opinions of this school, though possibly correct, are not self-evidently so. Thus, even if the Russians are always moving in a straight line towards that truth that all right-thinking men must consider obvious—a rash presumption in itself—the position and direction of that line are hardly unambiguous.

Also, we must consider the usual hiatus, common enough in our own country in all but exceptional times, between official military ideas, especially bold and advanced ones, and official political action. We must remember, too, that the milieu in which Soviet military ideas are formed and developed is totally different from ours, being much more confined to "responsible" circles of authority, and *that* is not likely to change soon.

Finally, and perhaps most important, changes of any kind in strategic ideas do not happen very fast. Often we can well afford to wait and see. If the

Edition of Marshal V. D. Sokolovskii's "Military Strategy," The RAND Corporation, RM-3972-PR, February 1964; Thomas W. Wolfe, *Soviet Strategy at the Crossroads,* Harvard University Press, 1964, and *Trends in Soviet Thinking on Theatre Warfare, Conventional Operations, and Limited War,* The RAND Corporation, RM-4305-PR, December 1964.

Russians are really going to develop a doctrine that would make the often spoken of "Hamburg grab" kind of strategy on their part conceivable (that is, a sharply delimited attack to capture that city made by conventional arms alone in defiance of our tactical nuclear power)—and it certainly is not conceivable under their present outlook—we are likely to be able to see the change coming a long way off. How much, then, should we anticipate it now?

One should no doubt also hedge predictive statements about future Soviet moves against the possibility that some technological breakthrough may alter in favor of the Soviets the current so-called strategic stalemate. One might notice, however, that inasmuch as what we now call "stalemate" is compatible with very great U.S. numerical and qualitative superiority, a break in the Russian favor that totally upset such a stalemate would have to be drastic indeed. If the Russians enjoyed the kind of superiority we presently enjoy they would probably behave differently from the way they are now behaving—especially with respect to Berlin. Thus, "stalemate" is partly a matter of who is superior to whom. Nevertheless, stalemate, as the term is normally used in this context, does seem to be inherently compatible with rather wide physical disparities. The Russians have after all not proved themselves to be enormously more clever and courageous than we, and the kind of situation that limits us would, if reversed, limit them as well.

Naturally, one does not wish to test this contention by yielding up our general superiority, which at the very least adds to our feeling of comfort. Nor does there seem to be any impelling reason at this time why we should have to.

Returning now to the initial proposition of this chapter: all of these considerations induce us to assign a far higher probability to the breaking out of conflicts on a small scale initially rather than on a grand scale, over issues that are relatively isolated, specific, and regionally limited. To repeat a point made earlier but important enough to bear repetition: it is a fairly safe prediction that from now on neither side will be able seriously and convincingly to use for political ends threats of strategic nuclear attack, or anything that in scale is even close to it. What one *can* threaten are lesser actions that *could* start events moving in that direction. The opponent cannot at any stage be deprived of the choice, within his capabilities, of making the situation more dangerous or less so; but we can reasonably hope and expect to influence his choices appropriately. This is what we must henceforth mean by deterrence, or by containing aggression militarily.

One therefore surmises that the military measures taken by us to cope with aggression, where we have assumed the responsibility for so doing, ought to have the following three general characteristics: They ought to be, so far as possible, (a) effective enough initially to prevent extensive deterioration

of the military situation, especially such deterioration as would basically alter the character of that
situation; (b) limited enough to leave unused, at
least temporarily, such higher levels of violence as
are not likely to be immediately necessary to accomplish the objective stated under (a)—levels
which must be most unattractive for the enemy to
enter; and (c) determined enough to show that we
are not more unwilling than he to move toward
those higher levels. One should notice that while
stipulation (a) asserts what is certainly desirable
even if not in all cases essential and (b) simply de-
fines limited war, it is (c) that establishes what *is*
essential to effective containment through limited
means. Without (c) we either lose outright or we
encourage the enemy to move to higher levels of
violence in which we avoid losing only by following him. It is obviously preferable to make clear to
him before he reaches for those higher levels that
it is dangerous for him to do so and will avail him
nothing.

BEFORE PROCEEDING further we must consider a theory or point of view that has received a good deal of emphasis, especially in the United States. It is by now easily identified by referring to the term "firebreak," in its special application to signify at the tactical level the barrier formed by the distinction between the use and non-use of nuclear weapons.[1] With that distinction frequently goes an advocacy, more or less intense, of the idea that maintaining it is all-important with respect to such matters as escalation, and that it is the only practicable distinction in sight upon which we can hope to base a policy of limitations in war. Thus, the "firebreak" is not only a phenomenon to be recognized but represents also an idea or conviction to be actively promoted, partly through preaching its merits to the unconverted both at home and abroad.

Let us first affirm that insofar as the term simply

[1] The first use known to me of the term "firebreak" in this connection was by Alain C. Enthoven, who has delivered a number of public speeches elucidating the theory or philosophy discussed in this chapter. A speech of his on this subject that won particular attention was one given before the Loyola University Forum for National Affairs, at Los Angeles, California, February 10, 1963. (Almost the whole of it is reproduced in the book of readings compiled by Henry A. Kissinger, *Problems of National Strategy*, Praeger, 1965, pp. 120-134.) I should add that certain cognate terms to express the general same idea are of much older use. I have myself referred to "the vast *watershed* of difference" between use and non-use of nuclear weapons in my *Strategy in the Missile Age*, Princeton University Press, Princeton, 1959; see especially p. 327.

connotes a belief that there is a profound difference in kind as well as in degree between nuclear
and non-nuclear weapons, almost every thinking
person must now subscribe to the firebreak idea.
The notion that the atomic bomb is "just another
weapon" was always flagrantly insensitive, even if
not wholly illogical. It was insensitive to the importance of a distinction, however arbitrary, that
most of the world was going to insist upon.

The fact that the United States did not use nuclear weapons in the Korean War was unquestionably due mostly to certain special circumstances
not likely to be repeated in the future.[2] Nevertheless, it did betray in addition a feeling that nuclear
weapons *were* different and that invoking their use
to any degree whatsoever, even when the tactical
situation was developing badly for us, must require a special and weighty decision. When President Truman, in a press conference during that
war, indicated that he and his advisers had been
"considering" their possible use in Korea, the British Prime Minister, Clement Atlee, rushed to Washington to persuade the President not to do so.

---

[2] I have described these special circumstances in *Strategy in the
Missile Age*, pp. 319f. Briefly summarized, the reasons were (a)
limited stockpile; (b) underestimation of the effects of nuclear
weapons against such tactically important objects as bridges; (c)
Pentagon and administration conviction that the North Korean
attack was a Soviet feint and that a Soviet attack in Europe was
impending, requiring conservation of limited bombs; (d) fears
and objections of our allies, especially Britain. The first three
of these cannot again occur. On the other hand, their non-use in
Korea did help to create what Thomas C. Schelling has called a
"tradition of non-use."

Whether the Prime Minister's anxieties made sense under the circumstances is quite beside the point. What mattered was that the mere mention of nuclear weapons by the President was enough to precipitate his trip, and that few people considered his behavior odd. We must, in other words, be aware that since the beginning of the nuclear era there has been in the minds of men a strong tendency to distinguish between nuclear and non-nuclear weapons, combined with a widespread fear of and aversion to the former, and this distinction and aversion have tended for a variety of reasons to grow stronger with time rather than weaker. Recognition of that important fact, however, is obviously distinct from the question of whether it is in the U.S. interest to advance, refortify, and universalize that distinction or on the contrary simply to accommodate to it, perhaps to the minimum degree possible. It might be reasonable to argue that the United States ought to seek by its words and acts to moderate or deflate the distinction, but it would hardly be reasonable to argue that we should simply ignore it.

It is important also to recognize that today, as distinct from the situation that existed throughout the decade of the fifties, a nearly universal consensus exists also within the ranks of professional military people that small military operations are simply out of bounds so far as concerns the use of nuclear weapons. How large such operations have to become before this particular consensus among the military dissolves into the opposing one would be difficult to ascertain—views would probably vary widely among individual officers—but we should recognize that the consensus against the use of nuclear weapons unquestionably extends over a fairly considerable and quite important zone of contingencies. Thus, on that issue there is no need to convert the already converted.

Let us also be clear that at present the United States, especially when acting together with her allies, already possesses a substantial non-nuclear capability, certainly one able to cope effectively with any quasi-accidental outbreak of fighting or small foray, either in Europe or in the Far East. If, for example, there were to be another Quemoy crisis like that of 1958, it is most doubtful that any voices would be raised, as some were then, to insist that we ought to intervene with nuclear weapons or not at all. The large conventional commitment to Vietnam in 1965-66 is proof enough of that.

These observations, on the other hand, are not likely to satisfy the more enthusiastic advocates of the firebreak idea, who usually insist that at the very least we should postpone any initiative in introducing nuclear weapons until a very high level of military operations is reached. Inescapably, this school has also advocated building up our conventional capabilities—and persuading our allies to do likewise—in order to be able to sustain a high level of conventional combat, that is, in order that we should not have to shift from conventional to nuclear weapons "out of weakness." The exact quantitative level that these advocates have in mind, which will of course vary with individuals, is less interesting, however, than some of the ideas that seem to be implicit and occasionally explicit in their arguments.

For example, the standard argument for rejecting as a useful "firebreak" any discrimination according to *size or character* of nuclear weapons is that it gives the enemy too much opportunity to mistake or deliberately exaggerate the size of the bombs one has used, and thus to proceed to use larger ones. However, one never senses in connection with this argument any inclination to question whether the enemy will *want* to do so, an issue that would surely override the question of his capacity to discriminate. He might very well want to do the opposite.

From various associated and familiar arguments, one may construct a model of the firebreak idea, as conceived by its more enthusiastic proponents, that usually seems to include at least the following assumptions:

(a) Inasmuch as the distinction between nuclear and non-nuclear weapons provides the only feasible firebreak in the area between outbreak of limited local hostilities and general war, both sides, insofar as it lies within their capabilities, will most likely not hesitate to outbid each other in violence *up to that limit.*

(b) Having reached that limit, both will be more or less equally grateful for its existence, and thus unready to consider further escalation.

(c) To attempt to place that kind of firebreak at a relatively low place in the scale of operations would subject it to an insupportable pressure such as would be missing—or which it could far better sustain—at high levels.

Obviously, this is not the kind of formulation that will be explicitly acknowledged or even accepted by the firebreak proponents. Yet it is hard to read anything else into an argument that relies so heavily on a mechanical barrier to prevent unwanted escalation rather than on the aims, intentions, or fears of the respective opponents, and that seems to place more faith on being able to avoid nuclear fighting if the tolerated magnitude of conventional fighting is placed at high levels rather than being confined to low ones. On the latter point especially, one can easily think of good reasons for suspecting the opposite.

It should also be noted that it is certainly a requirement for the feasibility of any firebreak notion, *especially one that envisages placing the barrier at a high level of tactical operations*, that the opponent should believe in it about as much as we do. Otherwise the whole environment for conventional fighting would simply be too precarious. For that reason advocacy of the firebreak idea entails not simply an expectation that the opponent can-

not be prevented from overhearing one's arguments
to friends and allies in favor of it. It entails rather
the keen desire, whether wholly conscious or not,
that he *should* overhear and be swayed by those
arguments.

It is on the other hand hardly possible to doubt
that the apparent rejection thus far of the firebreak idea by Soviet military theorists has worked
markedly to the advantage of the United States.[3] It
would otherwise be difficult to explain why the
Russians yielded so quickly and completely in the
Cuban crisis of October 1962. They obviously
feared to let a situation develop where one of our
destroyers might so much as fire a shot over the
bows of one of their transport ships. They clearly
wanted no fighting at all, apparently because they
felt that *any* fighting was extremely dangerous.
They were no doubt shrewder under the circumstances to act as they did, considering especially
President Kennedy's genuine and manifest resolution; but had they shared some current American
ideas they might have been willing to let things get
a good deal stickier before deciding to retreat.

It would similarly be hard to understand why
the development of the Cuban crisis resulted in an
immediate amelioration in the tension over Berlin,

[3] This point is indirectly confirmed by the firebreak proponents
themselves, who have often advanced as a primary reason for
building up conventional forces in Europe the possibility that
the Russians might attack westward with non-nuclear forces; this
the latter would presumably fear to do if they had to use nuclear
forces, or if they continued to hold the belief that any fighting
between them and us would quickly go nuclear.

with the Russians behaving themselves much better during and for a long time after the event than before. Clearly the Russians enjoyed local conventional superiority in and around the Berlin area, but they seemed not at all ready to test their local ascendancy on that basis. Raymond Aron, the distinguished French writer on political affairs, has several times pointed out that the United States and the Soviet Union each seems to favor strategic ideas more appropriate to the forces of the other, and that it is a great advantage to the West that the Russians seem unready to accept those special strategic ideas that are so popular in the United States.[4]

Naturally, there is no intention here of criticizing either the motives or the logical consistency of those who would induce the Russians (and Chinese) to accept fully the firebreak conception. On the contrary, it represents simply an honest conflict of goals and a reasonable (though I think incorrect) weighing of relative risk. The firebreak proponents seem to feel that the present anti-firebreak Soviet attitude *may* help deterrence but is much more dangerous to us if deterrence fails. For that reason they want to speed up Soviet acceptance of the idea, which they regard as inevitable anyway. One might in passing notice in this reasoning the interesting and marked differentiation between what are alleged to be deterrence interests and what are alleged to be war-fighting interests.

---

[4] See, for example, his *The Great Debate* (trans. from *Le grand débat*), New York, 1965, pp. 152-154.

One might also observe in passing that the Peking decision to intervene in the Korean War followed five months of watching us fight, sometimes desperately, without nuclear weapons—a fact which was unquestionably relevant and could have been important. The relevance is not really determined by whether or not the Chinese at that time seriously underestimated the power of nuclear weapons, which they very likely did, because our use of them might have served to disabuse them of their depreciating notions.[5]

This guessing about an historic incident relates to the more general and critical question of whether in the net it is in the American interest to promote further among our allies and the neutrals those distinctions between nuclear and non-nuclear weapons that are already so strong, or whether we should seek rather to soften them to some degree. Clearly, people representing the U.S. government have in recent years gone quite far in promoting the distinction. Much of this policy has been intended to induce our European allies to build up their conventional forces, in which respect our arguments have quite simply failed. The failure is perhaps regrettable. In any case we cannot avoid debating a question as important as this one on its merit.

[5] See Allen S. Whiting, *China Crosses the Yalu: The Decision to Enter the Korean War*, Macmillan, New York, 1960, pp. 134-136. Dr. Whiting is of the opinion that our non-use of nuclear weapons probably helped induce the Chinese to intervene.

WE MUST now consider the implications of the foregoing observations for our central subject: the problem of predicting the probabilities of uncontrolled escalation—or the dangers attending deliberate escalation—in the event of the outbreak of hostilities between either of the major Communist powers and the United States. We shall continue, however, to consider mainly the special case of Europe.

If the foregoing analysis is in essence reasonably correct, it should be clear that at least in Europe, wherever deterrence objectives diverge from either war-fighting or anti-escalation objectives, as they inevitably do in important ways, it would be seriously wrong to sell the former short. The appreciation that Europe is in all the important relevant respects entirely different from pre-1914 Europe, an appreciation which seems much rarer in the United States than among historically minded Europeans, justifies a kind of "going for broke" on deterrence that might have been irresponsible in an earlier age.

Actually, that is exactly the way in which the United States is proceeding on the strategic level. We have gone to great expense to build up a powerful and low-vulnerability strategic bombing system, the success of which will be measured

chiefly if not exclusively by whether or not it is
ever challenged. The dominant persuasion today
among defense specialists is that it faces little danger, at least in the near term, of being challenged.

Nevertheless, we have to assume that it is possible to imagine deterrence failing in Europe, and
we therefore have to consider what to do militarily
if it does. The first point to make, or to repeat, is
that it is impossible to consider intelligently what
to do if deterrence fails without at the same time
considering how and under what circumstances it
will have failed. This must be done in terms not so
much of the physical events themselves as of the
context of desires, aspirations, fears, and threats
affecting the two parties. It should be obvious, for
example, that Soviet behavior with respect to escalation will be affected one way if the Soviet Union
is reacting to a military initiative on our part, especially one that it considers a dangerous threat to its
very life, and quite another way if it sees us responding forcefully to its own aggressive moves at
relatively detached places like Berlin or Cuba.

To be sure, even in the latter cases the aggressor
may, in theory at least, be willing to take substantial risks to accomplish his ends. To be capable of
some disturbing act, some infringement on the
status quo, means at least to be other than wholly
wedded to the bliss of peace and quiet. This attitude may already sharply distinguish the aggressor
from his opponent. However, it is also possible
that the initiator of the disturbance may have cal-

culated that he faces no real risk of harm or loss, in which case the only real courage he is demonstrating by his act is the courage of a conviction that denies the existence of danger. He may expect the opponent to yield, or to compromise, or at the very minimum to go to some lengths to leave him an easy out. He may in fact be so firm in his conviction of the softness of the opponent that an initial act of resistance will not be enough to shake him; he will ascribe it to bluff. Nevertheless, such an aggressor is clearly not prepared to go very far in pursuing his object. The conviction that he can have something for nothing is inherently brittle, and bound (or at least *very* likely) to collapse quickly in the face of real determination.

Let us now imagine, as an example, the Russians firing at an American convoy which, after having been halted on the Berlin autobahn, has been ordered by its commander (acting upon higher orders) to continue on its way without awaiting permission. Or one could picture a similar case where the Russians put up a roadblock on the autobahn that American forces then proceed to destroy or to push out of their way.

If we assume—as we are bound to for most comparable cases in view of our present knowledge of the Soviet leaders—that they are anxious to avoid any war with us and certainly do not want one over Berlin, we can understand the Russians' being most unwilling to let this situation escalate. For this assumption carries also the corollary assumption that they will be not merely unwilling to persist but positively anxious to retreat if their probe provokes a suitably vigorous response from us.

Let us now make the added assumption that the issue over which the Soviets have stopped our convoy was an important one in which they feel themselves to be clearly in the right (for example, we have made a specific agreement with them over access rights which they feel we are now violating, or, more likely, we have previously let some of our prerogatives go to the Russians by default, but we are now trying to recapture some of them),[1] and let us assume also that we have a considerably more stubborn man, and one more confident concerning Soviet chances of prevailing, in control in the Soviet Union than either Khrushchev or his successors have thus far proved to be. Now we have a stickier situation to consider. The Soviet leaders are still anxious to avoid a real war with us, but they are not necessarily willing to retreat from their position the very moment some shots are exchanged. Let us assume further that both sides rush in such reinforcements as are locally available. Now we have a representative initiation of the so-called "inadvertent war," the kind nobody wants but which nevertheless breaks out.

---

[1] Our trying to recapture some convoy-passage prerogatives that we had needlessly let go by default created the convoy crisis of October 10-11, 1963. The situation was resolved by a "compromise" accommodation representing a net diplomatic loss by us as compared with earlier arrangements. The situation is well described by Jean Edward Smith, "Berlin: The Erosion of a Principle," *The Reporter*, November 21, 1963, pp. 32-37.

But what *has* broken out and how far has it gone? Both sides, we can imagine further, have remained in diplomatic contact (perhaps with "hot line" intact) or, if conceivably we must think of diplomatic relations having been ruptured before the circumstances described above, some substitute communications have been quickly developed. For the United States it would make a great deal of difference whether the Soviet action seemed to be designed to push us out of West Berlin or had a considerably lesser objective. The former issue is not negotiable, but others might be. If it remains our basic assumption that the Russians will not go to war over Berlin, we must make the corollary assumption that they are not ready to push us out. However, our leaders may not know that. One of the questions we should always be prepared to reexamine is: How much can U.S. political leaders be in doubt or in gross error about basic Soviet intentions? One merit of negotiations, incidentally, is that while they often fail to bring about a satisfactory agreement, they do sometimes help to clarify for each party what the other really wants—though it is often possible to know that quite well without negotiations, and sometimes the time allowable for negotiations is short.

The main question we are concerned with is the following: What are the circumstances that can really make such a situation as the one described above go out of control? It would seem that these circumstances boil down to two basic categories of factors, with various conceivable permutations and combinations of them. One of these is the prevalence of rigid mechanisms of military response, such as do tend or at least have tended in the past to pervade war-initiation concepts and also to get written into war plans. The other embraces that bundle of psychological factors summed up by (a) concern with loss of face and (b) tendencies to yield to feelings of hatred and rage.

The "rigid mechanisms" category is reflected in various common expressions about "pushing the button" or "the balloon going up." An interesting and possibly alarming aspect of the Cuban crisis of 1962 was the degree to which the crisis stimulated even among American administration leaders a tendency to think or at least to talk in such simplistic but absolute terms, despite the sophistication they had presumably been accumulating in the preceding months concerning the appropriateness of flexible response and the feasibility of limited operations. One has to be ready, it appears, for a kind of crisis-induced regression to older patterns of thinking about war and peace.

However, several things must be said on the other side. First, the fear of precisely such semi-automatic escalatory reactions on the part of the opponent acts as a powerful deterrent on both sides. Undoubtedly the degree of fear will be somewhat asymmetrical (which is *not* to say that it will likely be greater on our side). However, the present intensity of such fears among all the major powers suggests that the asymmetries are likely to be marginal and to be dominated by the circumstances of the occasion.

We are here again dealing with one of the ways in which the world, and especially that part of it which is Europe, is today strikingly different from what it was before 1914 or even 1939. We have historically been moving toward much higher levels of tolerance for types of behavior that previously would have been considered impossibly offensive, including limited acts of violence, which we are much readier than formerly to distinguish from acts of war. Also, all sorts of precautions and devices are being worked into the relevant systems—certainly on our side, and doubtlessly on the Soviet side as well—to keep military reactions from escalating spontaneously. It is more than a surmise, therefore, that the fears to which we have referred are counterescalatory at lower levels of violence, and that the levels at which automatic or spontaneous escalation may *tend* to take over are being pushed critically higher.

The other group of factors that we have referred to as possibly tending to stimulate uncontrolled escalation are the psychological ones, which, as we have seen, break down into two main sub-categories: (a) concern with saving face and (b) yielding to emotions like rage or fear.

An imputed universal preoccupation with saving face is probably the greatest single reason why most people assume so readily that resort to nuclear weapons must make for spontaneous escalation. We are all familiar with the normal human tendency to resist or rebel against letting the other fellow "get away with it," where "it" involves any deliberate blow or damage to our position or self-esteem. Also, among nations as among people—but usually more so—the word "prestige" covers a number of considerations ranging from mere vainglory to values of serious political moment. Damage to a nation's prestige can be a real injury in the sense that such damage may impose a cost on that nation—conceivably heavy and payable at some future time. This is especially true of military prestige, in which is bound up that image that other nations may entertain of one's rsolution as well as ability to fight effectively in what would generally be viewed as warranted circumstances.[2] One could easily give numerous examples, both historical and contemporary, of the reality of this consideration, but it should be hardly necessary to do so.

However, this is not the whole story. Nations are loath to suffer blows to their military prestige; yet they will normally suffer them in preference to suffering something worse. It is a question of imminent danger, pain, or penalty weighed (though not necessarily, or even usually, with cool and detached calculation) against possible future costs. The Soviet Union conspicuously backed down in Cuba in

---

[2] As Henry A. Kissinger has somewhere put it, "the 'domino theory' actually pervades all diplomacy."

October 1962, and the United States backed down to a considerable extent in Korea in 1951-52, when it quite clearly modified its earlier objectives as a result of Chinese intervention.[3] The degree of American accommodation in the latter instance was, as we have seen (pp. 17f.), not impelled by the military situation when negotiations began.

One of the most often repeated but nevertheless inane and historically unwarranted axioms about the behavior of nations in wartime is the familiar one that begins: "When one side finds itself losing, [etc.] . . . ," the usual implication being that then all stops are pulled—*nothing* is worse than defeat. This axiom was being advanced not long ago to explain why war could never be kept limited under any circumstances; more recently it has been used to explain why it is hopeless to expect a nation to refrain from using nuclear weapons in its possession when under extreme pressure on the battlefield. Although one instance does not prove much except the possibility of an exception, the United States refrained from using nuclear weapons while undergoing at the Yalu, in November-December 1950, one of the worst military defeats in its history, and that at a time when it enjoyed for all practical purposes a monopoly on such weapons!

---

[3] As late as September 30, 1950, Ambassador Austin had declared to the UN, "The opportunities for new aggression should be removed. . . . The aggressor's forces should not be permitted to have refuge behind an imaginary line. . . . The artificial barrier which has divided North and South Korea has no basis for existence either in law or in reason." See Whiting, *op. cit.*, p. 111.

Perhaps the main reason may have been that it did not have them ready for tactical use in that situation, but if so the lack of readiness is itself somewhat suggestive.

Concern with saving face is what each side tends primarily to attribute to the other. As Leites first pointed out more than a dozen years ago, old-line Communist leaders took great pains to inculcate in themselves the readiness to retreat when necessary without worrying about humiliation.[4] Naturally, the pretense of being greatly concerned with face may itself be a useful tactical maneuver. Naturally, too, the above-described precept, like most other precepts, is not likely to prevail in full or to remain unchanged—we are dealing after all with human beings—but one of the amazing demonstrations of the Cuban crisis was the degree to which Khrushchev appeared almost to rejoice in being able to demonstrate the classic Bolshevik precept that in a required retreat one must reject totally a concern with an attitude so puerile and so unworthy a professional revolutionary as humiliation. As Lenin had put it, in urging the necessity of capitulating to the Germans in March 1918, ". . . if you are not inclined to crawl in the mud on your belly, you are not a revolutionary but a chatterbox. . . ."[5] Khrushchev could probably have done much to conceal or minimize his humiliation—

[4] See Nathan Leites, *A Study of Bolshevism*, The Free Press, Glencoe, Ill., 1953, pp. 57-60, 491-503.
[5] Quoted *ibid.*, p. 499.

President Kennedy seemed quite ready to assist him in doing so—but the Soviet leader appeared to be little if at all interested in that objective; at least he seemed unwilling to take any risks at all in order to pursue it. Actually the Chinese Communists later flayed him for the precipitateness of his retreat (also for his initial "adventurism"), but they were ready to flay him on anything. What they actually criticized him for was the alleged lack of necessity for the hasty withdrawal (the United States being a "paper tiger") rather than for the "humiliation" of it.

We can also say of humiliation what we can say of reactions of rage—that governments, even Communist dictatorships, tend today to be corporate entities in which the emotional feelings of individuals, however highly placed, are likely to be moderated and contained by the counsels of their advisers. The Hitler regime was different and exceptional in this respect, though even Hitler, despite being much given to rages, seems rarely if ever to have made a really important political or strategic decision predominantly under the influence of that emotion. Where his decisions were irrational, they were so for reasons other than his fits of temper or rage.

Let us now imagine that a conflict has broken out involving American access to Berlin, and, with neither side willing to yield to the other, reinforcements have been run in by both sides and local fighting has intensified. We should notice again the point we have already alluded to—that one of the great drawbacks of following the so-called firebreak theory is that the more that confidence in the firebreak is built up, the less is each side restrained from committing larger and larger conventional forces within the limits of its capabilities. In other words, the effect is to stimulate escalation on the conventional side of the barrier, though fortunately, the location of that barrier is likely to remain ill-defined for sometime.

Let us now make the all-too-realistic assumption that the fighting described above takes place in a context in which the NATO partners have not succeeded in building up their conventional forces on the European central front to parity with the Russian forces. The Americans and their NATO allies now find themselves outnumbered on the ground, and the Russians, whose initiation of the action was probably without any clear desire to expel us from Berlin, perhaps begin to feel that it has now become possible for them to do so. The Americans, sensing this, decide to threaten the use of nuclear weapons. Perhaps the threat is, or promises to be, ineffective, and the U.S. government decides to use two or three such weapons as a demonstration of resolve—though with the understanding that the best way to demonstrate resolve is to use whatever bombs are used with the highest possible degree of military effectiveness. What is the likely Soviet response?

The common tendency in referring glibly to the

allegedly inherent "escalatory effect of nuclear weapons" is to assume that the Russians would react to this drastic American move by making the same kind of demonstrations, only with larger weapons and more of them. In the real world, however, we should have to ask with what misgivings and in fact utter dismay would the Russians now be contemplating such an act. To repeat, we are trying to describe a situation in which both sides were originally anxious to avoid hostilities and in which both certainly fear large-scale nuclear war. The Soviet Union is conscious that the existing dangerous situation has resulted from its own initiative, but it has been willing to barge ahead so long as (a) the fighting was still limited to conventional arms, in which it was not likely to suffer great damage, and (b) it could retreat from excessive danger in good time. How will it now resolve the question of how to respond to the opponent's unexpected resort to nuclear weapons?

We have in the present example left unclear the issue of particular responsibility for the outbreak of the fighting, but the Soviet Union remains aware that it is over an issue having to do with allied access to Berlin and not with something that deeply threatens her. Still, to proceed a step further in our speculations, let us imagine that the Soviet leaders nevertheless persist.

Perhaps they do feel it imperative for prestige reasons to make some semblance of a reply in kind, but if they decide to do so it will very likely be either because they still expect that the United States and its allies will back down or because the latter have communicated through some means their intention not to escalate further. In any case such a decision is immeasurably more likely to be the result of deliberate calculation, perhaps based on clear perception and good information and perhaps not, than of a compulsive urge to save face or vent their rage. Unless the Russians have what they must consider incontestable indication that we will yield first, they are acting with a kind of recklessness that they have not hitherto displayed in real life. Perhaps we too are acting with a courage unusual for us, but the question we are now putting to ourselves is this: What happens if we do so act?

It should also be observed that the situation described above has by no means reached a cataclysmic state, where everything goes up if the Russians decide to test us a little further. On the other hand, we should remind ourselves that the whole situation already appears markedly incompatible with our initial surmise (or stipulation)—that the Russians do not wish to become engaged in real fighting for the sake of getting us out of Berlin.

Let us therefore now alter our basic assumption and assert that the Russians *might be willing* to accept a limited war in Europe—even if there is risk of use or actual use of some nuclear weapons—for the sake of achieving its political objectives, because (a really necessary proviso) it is *quite con-*

fident that we will not push the issue to general war. This appears to be a most bold assumption, but we are only describing a kind of situation that is actually implied or posited in the once frequent talk about a possible large Russian attack against the NATO line on the central front. The questions we must ask at this point are: (a) Is it likely to be *feasible* for us to keep the ensuing fighting conventional? and (b) Is it *desirable* for us to attempt to do so or to appear eager to do so? We are now assuming the Russians are bent on aggression, and can bring themselves to accept the tactical detonation of a score of nuclear weapons, perhaps even considerable more.

If we are to be at all consistent with some of our previous assumptions, we have to assume also a fair to good chance that even if we do not use nuclear weapons but somehow manage to resist effectively, the Russians will themselves introduce nuclear weapons. Our present basic assumption, after all, *is that they have accepted the risks entailed in large-scale aggression,* which *must* include in their minds the risk that *we* will use nuclear weapons. How can they exclude that risk? If, nevertheless, with battle joined, they now see us by our restraint signalling our desperate desire to avoid the use of such weapons, they are open to some new thoughts. From this demonstration they might well deduce that we must be markedly less willing than they to withstand any use of nuclear weapons.

Perhaps they will not make that deduction; but

how can we then assume that they will be more willing to accept defeat (or even stalemate) in a battle that has remained conventional than in one that has gone nuclear? Is it not a compelling surmise—since the assumption is that they have committed themselves to large-scale aggression—that it must be just the other way around? Thus it would seem that under the admittedly unrealistic premises we have set for ourselves (in terms of Russian readiness for nuclear risk-taking) the best way, perhaps the only way, for us to avert not only defeat but unnecessary escalation is to demonstrate clearly that our readiness to take risks is not less than theirs. How can we do that except by using the weapons—demonstratively, few rather than many, and in as controlled a manner as possible, but nevertheless rather more abruptly than the Russians seem to have bargained for in launching their aggression?

Another and final notion that we will here consider, not because it makes a great deal of sense but because it has been very frequently encountered, is that the Russians might launch a deliberate large-scale aggression against us without planning to use nuclear weapons or wishing to do so but prepared to retaliate in kind and to at least comparable degree if we use them. This idea thus assumes that the Russians will, according to the old code of the duel, blithely leave us to the "choice of weapons" while remaining committed to fighting either way! However, we can permit the additional assumption that they strongly expect that we will not use them.

Even so, admitting also the latter assumption, under any circumstances remotely like those existing today this example assumes "adventurism" of really fantastic proportions, totally out of line with any behavior of theirs that we have witnessed in the past. Nevertheless, we must force ourselves to try to think the situation through a little further. How do we cope in advance with the conceivability of such an attack?

An answer often heard until recently (and by no means dead as a conviction) is that we must anticipate it by building up our own and allied conventional forces, thus deterring the enemy from starting his fight. But to this argument the premise is *essential* that the opponent either (a) is prepared to fight even with nuclear weapons or (b) is utterly convinced that we will not use them under any circumstances. Otherwise, he will certainly not let himself be provoked into attacking our forces with their large tactical nuclear capabilities. If he is prepared to fight with nuclear weapons, but observes from our costly efforts to build up to conventional parity with him in Europe that we are deeply unwilling to see them used, his cue, to repeat, is to threaten their use or actually to introduce a few. But if one insists that he will not do so, in other words that the portion (a) of the premise above does not apply, why should we permit and even encourage the conviction described under the portion (b), and what could a large conventional buildup buy us in addition to the encouragement of that conviction? We have not even asked whether the Soviet Union would fail to keep pace with us or outpace us in such a buildup, it being after all a sphere in which they enjoy, to put it mildly, the least comparative disadvantage.

We have to remind ourselves once more that we have in these speculations deliberately bestowed upon the Soviet leaders a far far greater spiritual or rather intestinal capacity for aggression than they have yet shown evidence of. We have also left open the question of whether our own leaders could marshal the necessary psychological resources to introduce the use of nuclear weapons and to out-bid any Soviet use. Perhaps they will not have that capacity, in the real world of the future. But it is one thing to be forced to admit that we could not, and quite another to say we should not. Nor should we confuse the issue by accepting the argument that we should not *because* we could not. It would at this stage in time be a most hazardous assertion to make that in *the event of blatant and major Soviet aggression against our forces in Europe* we could not bring ourselves to use tactical nuclear weapons. Anyway, if we could not, we would be in a bad way for defending Europe against Soviet aggression (*if* the Soviet Union were really that aggressive). We certainly could not solve the problem by securing from our allies and contributing ourselves to a buildup to conventional parity with the Russians. To build up conventional forces *be-*

cause we feel we dare not use nuclear forces even against a major attack is only to underline and to signal weakness. True, the opponent may not be alert to that signal because of his own deep and abiding fear of nuclear weapons. If so, good; then he will not attack. But we really ought to decide it one way or another. We cannot and ought not go on assuming a Soviet Union bent on major aggression but afraid of using nuclear weapons.

Our brief speculations have encompassed only cases in which a relatively small number of nuclear weapons are used more or less in demonstrations. There could be variations on this theme, including fairly wide use of small and highly specialized weapons—but the essential issue is maintaining tight control. Is this a grave weakness of these speculations? Not within the assumptions that we have found most realistic, which state simply that both sides share a common determination to avoid going into an exchange bound to be many, many times more costly than any imaginable political goal could justify and also that both sides can and will avoid utterly losing their heads. Drop those assumptions and we are inevitably back in the world of massive retaliation. If it should happen to be the case that existing war plans do not accord with our best thinking in these matters, they can in time be suitably altered—as they have been in the past.

If we turn now to the Far East, we see that the situation is different in certain vital respects. For one thing, we have fought a fairly large war on the

Korean peninsula without once using nuclear weapons that were in our possession. We have thus set a pattern for enemy expectations, as well as for our own. Secretary Dulles's verbal effort to change those expectations never had much strength, and is by now largely dissipated. Meanwhile we have gotten ourselves deeply involved in Vietnam, where, as already observed, there is not likely to be occasion for actual use of nuclear weapons.

The Chinese Communists obviously have little nuclear capability now, and will not have a substantial one for a long time to come. In this situation, where the risk of unwanted escalation hardly exists for us, we could stay conventional in a conflict with them just because the enemy would be quite willing to let us do so. Or possibly we may feel that there is less prestige or other value to be lost from defeat in that part of the world than from defeat in Europe. Perhaps even some romantic (that is, morbid) spirit of fair play might prevent us from dropping nuclear bombs upon an enemy who does not have many, precisely because he does not have many and is therefore almost certain to leave the decision for going nuclear entirely up to us. Also we are restrained by the firebreak idea, which permits few if any distinctions between regions of the world. What undermines it in one place admittedly undermines it everywhere.

It is therefore quite possible that we could fight another war in the Far East as large as the Korean War, or even a repetition of that war, without using nuclear weapons—assuming the American people permitted the government to engage again in such a war. Probably we could even prevail on that basis, as we did militarily in the previous Korean War (only to discard our advantages when entering negotiations by halting the then ongoing offensive that was succeeding brilliantly and that was our major leverage upon the opponent).[6] But surely it would be going about the job the hard way, especially since timely indication of readiness to use nuclear weapons is *bound* to have an enormous, and very likely a guaranteed, deterrent power.

Failure to use them under such circumstances would probably have repercussions for the future that would in the net be not to our liking. If the Chinese should manage to fight two substantial wars with us during the first three or four decades of the nuclear age without suffering exposure to a single nuclear weapon, we will have fixed for them a pattern which they have every further incentive to exploit.

The gigantic nuclear capabilities of the United States have already been appreciably cut down in their effectiveness as deterrents by what might be called established world opinion (including our own) opposed to their use. To a large extent this has been inevitable and, because it was right to dissociate ourselves from the "just another weapon" philosophy, even desirable. Perhaps too it is a necessary part of the price we pay for attempting to

[6] See *Strategy in the Missile Age*, p. 318; also above, pp. 17f.

restrain nuclear proliferation. But it behooves us to examine far more carefully than we have thus far some of the main propositions and arguments commonly made in support of our own drive to push even further toward what must in effect be the psychological neutralization through self-denial of our tactical nuclear capabilities.

In the above exercise we have examined particularly those arguments which emphasize the alleged escalatory potential of any and all uses or threats of use of nuclear weapons. If our considerations have been as yet too lean and circumscribed to serve in themselves as a basis for major policy recommendations, they have perhaps succeeded in making the point that some of the arguments upon which major policy recommendations have in fact been based are extraordinarily vulnerable to systematic analysis. They may also have helped to point out the directions in which it is both feasible and desirable to pursue additional relevant analysis.

If it be charged that we have not really faced up to the awful risks inherent in miscalculation, or in the tendency to madness that sometimes seems to go with resort to violence, the answer can only be that risks are something we have to measure as best we can. The above essay is an effort to contribute to such measurement. We cannot forfeit the task simply by allowing in advance such gross exaggeration of the risks as to "play it safe." A second look may quickly inform us that we do not really add to our safety by doing so.

APPENDIX

The Intractability of States:
A Distinctive Problem*

HAVING MORE than the usual number of psycho-analysts among my friends and acquaintances, and being rather exposed to their thoughts on many subjects,[1] I was led to interpret the subtitle of the subject for this panel—"Influencing an Intractable Adversary by Non-Violent Means"—in a way which I hope is not entirely inept.

The wording of this subtitle smacks of the clinic. One pictures a psychologically astute and emotionally well-ordered physician treating a deeply disturbed patient who is intractable. We know that it is a mark of competence in such a physician that he is able to do so by non-violent means.

But what kind of non-violent means? Perhaps the main title gives us further clarification. Here we find the rather startling words: "Pacifism, Martyrdom, and Appeasement." These words signify something not merely non-violent, but definitely passive and even masochistic. They seem to betoken

---

* This paper was prepared for a panel on "Pacifism, Martyrdom, and Appeasement: Dealing with Intractable States by Non-Violent Means" which is part of the annual conference of the American Psychological Association. It was presented at the Statler Hilton Hotel in Los Angeles on September 7, 1964.
[1] I happen also to be on the Board of Directors of the Foundation for Research in Psychoanalysis, in Los Angeles.

not a triumph over violence but rather a surrender to it. The word "pacifism" implies a refusal to discriminate according to types of and purposes for violence, it is a rejection of all violence; "martyrdom" suggests the not-too-unwilling victim of violence; and "appeasement" simply means to assuage the potentially violent one by giving him what he wants, presumably whatever he wants.

It is obvious that one could easily fill one's allotted twenty minutes with a discussion of any one of the words mentioned in this title. However, I have chosen to address myself to the imagery provoked by the subtitle, especially its suggestion of person-to-person contact. This suggestion is indeed reinforced by the main title, the first two words of which surely tend to reflect individual and personal rather than state behavior.

If we speak about influencing an "intractable" adversary, it makes an enormous difference whether we are speaking about a person or about a government of a great nation. Governments are of course made up of persons, and we have reason for feeling that we have by now learned a great deal about the behavior of persons. Especially in our own century, with its deep exploration of the realm of the unconscious, we have advanced to the point where we feel we understand most of the salient features of human conduct, even if we do not always know how to correct its ills. However, I think it is important to realize that we know very little about the influence of personal psychology on the behavior of states. Despite the promising beginnings made some thirty years ago by Harold D. Lasswell and others, who attempted to bring to the study of politics, including international politics, the then relatively novel and revolutionary insights of psychoanalysis, the indicated kinds of research have even by now scarcely been undertaken.

But surely, one might argue, the political behavior of a state is a direct result of the decision-making processes of the persons who control the state and speak for it. Do we not know that these persons have the normal human endowment of aggression, and sometimes an abnormal one? Can we not guess that there is likely to be among the leaders of states a good deal of repressed rage looking for an outlet, as well as assorted complexes of juvenile fears which warp one's perspective and judgment? May we not suppose that if we could properly screen the persons who reach supreme or even important office, or could exercise beneficial therapy upon them, then we could perhaps begin to realize the kind of mature, wise, tolerant, and confident behavior among states which is our image of the ideal clinician's behavior in the psychopathic ward. If we could be sure that those who governed us were emotionally sound and mature, would not our worries all be over?

I am all for having that kind of person in high office. I have, incidentally, the feeling that our democratic processes on the whole work pretty well in bringing to the top the kinds of persons who are generally healthy psychically rather than the reverse. Certainly the conspicuous examples of the reverse that we have seen in recent times have been in the dictatorships we have known rather than in the democracies. However, I also think that even if we could materially improve by appropriate selective and also therapeutic processes the psychic and emotional equipment of those who govern us, we would have moved a relatively small distance toward curing or even materially improving the situation we have in mind when we speak of problems of war and peace.

In the decision-making processes that account for the political behavior of states, we observe conspicuously at work many factors that greatly modify the emotional and other psychological elements which so directly influence individual behavior, including the behavior of the statesman. Most obviously, the actions of states stem characteristically from decisions reached by groups rather than by individuals. Even Senator Barry Goldwater, who is not yet a leader of a great nation but only aspires to be one, is already a corporate entity.[2] He was actually that even before he became an official candidate. He became so by accumulating a battery of ghost writers, advisers, and other cohorts of varying degrees of intimacy. Sometimes the lonely man behind it all speaks out for himself, and thus becomes momentarily visible as a perhaps strikingly

[2] This paper was prepared during the presidential election campaign of 1964.

different kind of person from what we have been led to believe, but for the most part he is conforming to an image which his whole organization is projecting and of which he is only one of the architects. I do not mean that all candidates or statesmen exist in this same kind and degree of corporate establishment—we are familiar with the phenomenon of individual style, which distinguishes the administration of one president from that of his predecessor or successor, and of course we know that the man at the top makes the choices (though with less than complete freedom) of those who will assist him, at least at high levels—but from then on he works with them and through them.

Another conspicuous difference is that in the interaction of states, the time factor between stimulus and response is generally longer, often much longer, than in the interaction of persons. We admire the politician who is quick on his feet in a press conference or on the hustings, but this is an irrelevant trait when he is functioning as the leader of a state dealing with the leaders of other states.

There is thus little counterpart among states to the verbal or physical slap in the face which is sometimes experienced by persons and which usually provokes various types of quick and violent behavior. It is of course obvious that statesmen may feel anger at the actions of other states, which is to say at the public behavior of those who govern those states, and sometimes that emotion is effective in influencing their response. Sometimes too the amount of time available for response is relatively constricted.

A good example, I think, was the crisis of June 1950 that caused President Truman to decide that the United States must intervene to assist the South Koreans against the shockingly bald aggression from the Communist north. No doubt President Truman was angry, as were, I am sure, many of those around him, and there is little doubt that this feeling acted to some extent as a galvanizing agent in the series of moves that brought about the decision to intervene. Also, the attack had come as a great surprise, and there was therefore little time in which to decide what to do. But it is nevertheless quite clear that President Truman sought and obtained the advice of various people around him, that the time allowed for decision was measured in hours and days instead of seconds or minutes, and that calculations of interest and the likely consequences following from various kinds of alternative responses were to some degree investigated and appraised. It is no doubt correct to say that some degree of anger played a part in determining the policy actually pursued, but it would be not only a libel against President Truman but also a great historical error to say that he acted only or even predominantly out of anger.

If we look at the handling of the Cuban crisis of October 1962, we see even more conspicuously the operation of the corporate entity which was the President and his staff—several concentric rings of

influence around the center of decision, including
even the lower ranks in parts of the Washington
bureaucracy. Also, that there was a period of about
a week before the crisis broke in which a policy
could be hammered out from among the various
alternatives that had been checked over. One observes fragments of evidence of personal strain as a
result of the week of serious tension, but the whole
episode takes on more the appearance of a well-
oiled and carefully built-up machine responding to
a task for which it was designed than of a person
full of hurt and grievance responding to the treach-
erous move of a personal adversary.

My two examples also point to another enormous
difference between the behavior of states and that
of individuals. In the case of the North Korean attack, the adversary was not a person but a complete abstraction. It was not even an entity known
as the government of North Korea but rather an
even more abstract one known as World Communism with the center of control—at that time at
any rate—in Moscow. Even in the Cuban crisis the
adversary was an abstraction, though admittedly
less so. Certainly it was not considered to be Mr.
Khrushchev alone. Our administration seemed in
fact to be assuming, probably wrongly, that there
was a play for power on the part of competing
groups within the Kremlin, and that it was incumbent upon us in our responses to help the more
reasonable and peace-loving group rather than the
alternative. This attitude seemed to play a con-

siderable part in our decisions, even though the persons in the Kremlin who were supposed to be the respective parties of war and peace could not be identified by us. We were dealing with an abstraction of which Mr. Khrushchev seemed at times to be only a small and beleaguered part. Some apparently even looked upon him as our friend in the Kremlin, the benign fellow whom we had to protect from "those others." I must stress that it is still not known publicly to what degree this kind of thinking prevailed in Washington, but it clearly seems to have played a part.

Obviously too, the confrontations of Korea and Cuba were not of the face-to-face character so often characteristic of personal relations and so important a factor in those relations. Negotiations were carried on over thousands of miles of separating distance, by varying forms of communication, apparently with interesting side-line contacts between intermediaries which helped to determine the kinds of letters that were written and exchanged between the heads of government. President Kennedy had once met Chairman Khrushchev in Vienna shortly after the former took office, but this meeting seems to have had quite negative results not only as to reaching any agreement but also by giving each principal a rather wrong impression of the other. After all, wrong impressions of another can often survive long and fairly intimate association.

Perhaps most important of all, governmental behavior is modified not only by the cultural milieus but also by the national traditions and by the distinctive political precepts which may characterize each of the several parties to the confrontation. Certainly in each of the examples I have given, our government was dealing with an adversary whose avowed political precepts, goals, and modes of behavior were quite different from ours. Since one of the major precepts of behavior in the Bolshevik code is that personal feelings, whether of fear, rage, humiliation and the like, must be utterly controlled and rejected as influences upon one's political conduct—I am not suggesting that they always succeed in following that very stern injunction, but it is surely important that they consciously try—it is very important that those who advise our policy-makers in their dealings with the Communist nations should have considerable familiarity with the Communist operational code.

All this is not to say that the psychological make-up of our own policy-makers, especially those of the top level, is unimportant. It is only to say that we must beware of generalizing too easily from the area of personal behavior to that of government.

Thus, for learning how to deal with states led by difficult or hostile governments, clinical experience with intractable patients is not only unlikely to be of help, but insofar as we are inclined to be literal about transposing lessons from one milieu of operations to the other, it is certain to be deceptive. The intractability of states is sure to be a totally different phenomenon from that of individuals, both in predisposing factors and in operational purpose.

It is therefore misleading to speak of the behavior of governments toward each other as being "paranoid," as is sometimes done, even when that behavior is indeed full of suspicion and hostility. Genuine paranoia among persons is often hard to detect, even after long acquaintance, but in any case the word "paranoia" or "paranoid" implies in the individual a burden of suspicion and hostility that is quite unjustified by the objective facts. It is probably true that Mr. Khrushchev's attitude and behavior toward us is in large part inspired by a wrong impression of us, and I don't doubt that something of the same sort works in the opposite direction as well. But it also appears that these misapprehensions derive from something other than psychopathology. That something else is, on the Communist side, a quasi-religious and dynamic ideology, which affects both their goals and the kind of perception they have of us. We are bound to be opposed to their goals, and also to have special problems in interpreting what is after all a system extraordinarily different from ours.

The resulting misperception and misjudgment are obviously completely compatible with having men in power on both sides who are about as healthy psychically as anyone could reasonably expect them to be. There is not the slightest evidence to suggest that Chairman Khrushchev is at all paranoid, and it seems clear that neither is President Johnson. The suspicion that each has of the other has some real justification, and improvement of the strictly personal knowledge each has of the other would not in itself reduce or moderate this suspicion. Obviously there is something wrong in all this, because both countries would be better off with a different kind of "intergovernmental" behavior. But I think improvement depends on advancing our political at least as much as our psychological understanding (unless each is so broadly conceived as to include the other).

Are we therefore to assume that psychology has little to contribute in improving our understanding of the relations between states, and especially of the optimum means of avoiding violence between states? I think it has a very great deal to offer, but I think also that the area in which we can hope to receive the most instruction is not that in which we directly examine the relations between states. I think the profitable area is rather that of the relations of individuals within each state, especially those factors that account for the rise to power and to influence of particular persons, groups, and cliques, and which determine how those persons or groups exercise their power and the devious and usually extremely subtle ways by which individual psychic quirks can get translated into foreign policy. I am simply making the obvious point that, psychology being a science dealing with *human* behavior, we should look for it to be most germane and rewarding in those areas in which human beings interact as persons rather than as corporate and abstract entities called governments.

Concerning the relation of states with each other, especially with reference to how wars may be avoided, I should suggest that there are at least two fields, one of them pretty far removed from psychology, where gaining additional knowledge is all to the good and where the availability of expert knowledge is indispensable. I refer first to the importance of understanding the character of state power, meaning primarily military power, and what its uses and limitations are in achieving the major ends of state power. One of the first of these ends is certainly, for us, the maintenance of peace without the sacrifice of important values or without accepting any ultimate degradation of our position. The genuine pacifist turns his back on power in a world in which governments hostile to our own use power to pursue what even he, the pacifist, must acknowledge are inimical goals. I think that is why the pacifist has been generally ineffective in our time. He refuses to have anything to do with that power, which, when correctly developed and well handled can account for the favorable resolution of a crisis like that over the missiles in Cuba in 1962, in the sequel of which it is hard to detect any important flaw. Many persons at the time were shocked at the very idea of confrontation, which seemed somehow to spell diplomatic failure as well as to present a great danger. Let us also not forget with respect to that crisis the grand importance of our marked overall superiority over the adversary, which among other things helped to give our leaders the necessary resolution and confidence, especially since they knew that the adversary was aware of our great superiority.

It is often important to know what kind of confrontation to make and how, when one is made, to appraise its results. If the airlift during the Berlin blockade of 1948 may be considered a non-violent means of dealing successfully with the intractable opponent, what could or should we have done if that airlift had proved unfeasible? Was it wise to resort to the airlift rather than to insist on our rights to ground access? The answers to such questions are certainly not obvious.

The other equipment that I think we need, sometimes desperately, in order to help us avoid war while dealing effectively with intractable adversaries is a thorough knowledge of the special idiosyncrasies of that adversary. Notice that means knowledge of the adversary not primarily as a human being or group of human beings but as a complex of people organized as a state with distinctive political institutions. We want to know, among other things, the interpretations that an opponent widely removed from us in culture and in political doctrine will put upon our actions. Those interpretations may be very different from what we think a reasonable person ought to put on them, but the differences are of a nature that experts can often estimate shrewdly. I referred earlier to the opinions that seemed to be current during the Cuban crisis in our own government concerning the nature of the adversary, especially that school of thought which insisted on seeing in the Kremlin a struggle between contending groups where the outcome could probably be determined by our behavior. Was that a correct interpretation? For the short term it was almost certainly not.[3]

I am suggesting that the kind of knowledge that is represented in our country in the work of a handful of Soviet experts is in most instances absolutely indispensable to correct action vis-à-vis the Soviet Union. A few of these experts happen also to have considerable psychological insight, and perhaps know how to use it to advantage. But one notices that the advantages gained from this kind of insight, while important, are not necessarily commanding. The expert uses other kinds of equipment much more, especially the kind that perfects his image of the opposing head of state as a part of a highly idiosyncratic political apparatus.

[3] It is more than doubtful whether Krushchev's fall from power more than two years after the event had very much to do with the outcome of the Cuban crisis. The very considerable lapse of time would in itself argue against it, but there are other reasons.

Index

Made in the USA
Coppell, TX
02 January 2023